Flyin
for
Kaiser Wilhelm

ACES AEROPLANES AND DEFEAT

Kaiser Wilhelm II June 1906

the Emperor of Germany

Unteroffizier Ernst Udet and Lo Zink
whom he married after the war

"You carry a black cross on your wings and others a cockade, but in both machines sit our sons." M. Fernand to Udet

Fraulein Melli Beese Germany's first woman pilot

Flying
for
Kaiser Wilhelm

C. Barrowman (Ed.)

ACES AEROPLANES
AND
DEFEAT

Publisher: A.MacKay (Publisher) Ltd

ISBN: 978-1-8380567-5-9 Editor: C. Barrowman

Research/Translator: C.E. MacKay/Allan Morrison

Set in Times New Roman, 16 Point, A4 by the publisher and printed in A5 by Merchant City Print

CONTENTS

An Early Balloon Flight

Lieutenant Albert Willy Richter, the son of Colonel Lieutenant Richter, was born on 9 December 1886 in Zittau, then a garrison city. He attended school there until 1896. By 1900 he had attended high schools partly in Chemnitz, partly in Döbeln and then the Prince School in Grimma by Easter 1900. He attended the Grimma School for six years. In 1906 after passing his high school exams in Grimma he became a cadet in the 12th K. S. Infantry Regiment 177 in Dresden. Richter then attended the Glogau war school completed his course and graduated in July 1907 and was promoted to lieutenant in the same regiment that year.

On Saturday, the 19 December 1909, at 4:30 p.m. in the Balloon "Luna" at Weissig near Dresden, he planned to ascend on a long distance balloon flight to near the Baltic Sea. Today he was going to fly "Luna" from Dresden to Danzig. In this case he was alone and intended to fly on a night trip. In the basket he had warm clothing, tinned food, life belts and 32 bags of ballast.

When he ascended the board of directors of the Dresden Airship Association were very concerned due to the wind blowing from a south westerly direction. On the Friday the balloon was seen heading north showing the Saxon colours. He flew low and then headed for Geta, Richter was clearly visible in the basket. Possibly he was heading for the Aaland Islands in the Baltic Sea. By the Tuesday no news had been received from him and the Association sent out messages to Stockholm, Christiana, Copenhagen and Helsinfors asking for information. They also contacted the German Foreign Office asking at their Embassies in Stockholm, Christiania, Saint Petersburg and Copenhagen to make further enquiries: - nothing was heard. By now the Association was offering 1000 Marks for information on Lieutenant Richter and the balloon Luna but it was felt he had disappeared into the Baltic Sea.

On 7 February 1910 news was received in Dresden that an empty balloon basket had been sighted in the sea off Jakobstad, Finland. The Dresden Airship Association concluded that it was the balloon Luna and that Lieutenant Albert Willy Richter had been lost.

(Translated)

Preface

On completion of *German Aircraft in the Great War* there was much surplus material left that could not be included in that book due to size. It was then decided to produce a companion to the first volume using the surplus information that had been researched. Included here are biographies of pilots, more aeroplane details and illustrations, information on armament, the balloon service and the position of German wartime aeroplanes absorbed by the Entente forces at the Armistice and their disposal. Also included are the circumstances surrounding the Armistice of November 1918 and the fate of the Emperor and the Crown Prince. All has been included in its original form –"*ne prorsus interirent*" – lest they utterly perish.

Britain and France had come to a pre-war agreement called "*The Entente Cordiale*," an understanding brokered by the British King, Edward VII in 1904. When war broke out in August 1914 the German wartime position was initially successful but culminated in tragedy; Germany misjudged the industrial capacity of the Entente and its ability to draw on the manpower of Empire. The German forces were outgeneralled, outmanoeuvred and out-resourced by August 1918 and defeated resulting in the myth of, "*The stab in the back,*" believed by the German military. The Armistice and the draconian Treaty of Versailles of 1919 meant that Germany was also not allowed to have an air force and her military forces were severely curtailed.

The German population and minorities were blamed for the loss of war and the cry of this myth was taken over by the Nazi Party and grown out of all proportion. The Americans under General Pershing wanted to take the war into Germany but the Armistice stopped the advance but the defeat of 1918 was nothing compared to the defeat that was to come in 1945 when Germany lost everything.

All place names and names in this publication; facts and figures are taken from contemporary documents, including intelligence reports and these have not been changed.

Researchers Notes

The key research publication was part of the A.S.N. Gritton collection, "The Waverly History of the Great War" etc. and a single bound volume of a weekly publication printed with a dark cover and "The Great War" in gold lettering on the cover. Other parts of this collection were "Twenty Years After" and others. These publications were filled with facts and profusely illustrated. This was followed by research in the Mitchell Library and the use of their internet search provider, Pro-Quest and the use of the publisher's archive and the C.E. Mac Kay collection. Assistance was received earlier from the late J.M. Bruce and Chaz Bowyer. J.M. Bruce provided Profiles on German aircraft, armament and other information on intelligence papers of the German Air Force and where they could be located. Many of these documents were in French or German and had to be manually translated. Most of the information gleaned by the Entente intelligence service came from prisoners. That information was obtained in the relevant national archives. This was time consuming.
The Mitchell Library has an excellent patent collection but they can also be viewed at *Espacenet.com*

An internet search provided contemporary newspapers and magazines which were full of information. Some modern information did not fit the contemporary details so the contemporary details were used. The family oral tradition was also very strong at this historical point for 1918. We were told of pamphlets being left behind by the German army declaring the army was let down by the German population particularly the German Jews. These declarations were confirmed in the memoirs of the leading German generals and admirals. The German minority parties grasped these details with a vengeance resulting in the growth of the National Socialist Party and the German popularity of Adolph Hitler.

Netherton *24 March 2023*

Acknowledgement

Many thanks to the Mitchell Library, Glasgow for professional assistance and guidance, Librarian and staff at Bishopbriggs library, the Librarian Royal Aeronautical Society, United Nations Library-SOCIÉTÉ DES NATIONS, United States Archives, Smithsonian Institute, United States Air Force Museum, Library of Congress, Australian War Memorial, local studies team at West Dumbarton Council, formerly Clydebank District Council, the Aviation Bookshop Tunbridge Wells for information etc. To the late J.M. Bruce and Chaz Bowyer for information and assistance: the MacKay family for the use of information, access to their contemporary collection and use of their oral tradition, Rolls-Royce Heritage Trust, Scottish Branch, the Laloe family, to C. Barrowman for her enthusiasm for the project and her input and to family and friends for their encouragement and guidance helping to finish the project. All conclusions and translations are by the researchers and they apologise for any mistakes which occur.

CM/AM *28 March 2023*

Aviators

On the left Leutnant Vierlin and on t right Leutnant Canter. Both at the flying school Doberitz 1911. Vierlin became a test pilot at the Bavarian fighter test centre. Canter became famous for his reconnaissance flight 30 August 1914 when, as a pilot in Feldflieger Abteilung 14, he brought important information on the positio and strength of Russian forces durin the Battle of Tannenberg

Leautnant Eisenmenger (right) and Vice Sergeant Gund (left), whilst dur an observation flight over the lines o 23 May 1918 shot down six Sopwith Camels.

Max Immelmann the Eagle of Lille

Erwin Böhme (29 July 1879 – 29 November 1917), was a fighter ace credited with 24 aerial victories and was a renowned traveller and Alpinist. After serving in a bomber unit, he was transferred to Germany's first fighter squadron Jagdstaffel 2. During Böhme's combat career, he was a friend and eventual subordinate to Manfred von Richthofen, the Red Baron. He was also friend, subordinate and wingman to Germany's leading ace of the time, Oswald Boelcke. Böhme was inadvertently responsible for Boelcke's death on 28 October 1916. He was shot down in his Albatros D.Va on 23 November 1917.

Leutnant Max Ritter von Mulzer (9 July 1893 - 26 September 1916) was credited with ten aerial victories. He was the first Bavarian fighter ace, first Bavarian ace recipient of the Pour le Merite and first Bavarian knighted for his exploits. On 26 September 1916, he had a new aircraft to test fly an Albatros D.1. He took off from the Valenciennes airfield on a test flight, side-slipped his Albatros D.I into a hard bank, lost control and crashed to his death.

Eduard-Maria Joseph Ritter von Schleich born Schleich (9 August 1888 – 15 November 1947), in the cockpit of his Albatros, was a high scoring Bavarian flying ace. He was credited with 35 aerial victories by the end of the war.

Major, later lieutenant Colonel Siegert, was inspector of the Air Force from 1916 and laid down the training guidelines and policy and had great influence on the development of the German Air Force. In 1915 he was 2nd Staff Officer of Field Air Services (1915–1916) and Inspector of Flying Troops (1916–1918).

Paul Engelhard in flight at Johannisthal, Berlin, 12 August 1910.He was the first to fly in Switzerland and there he used a Wright machine.

Oberleutnant Eduard Ritter von Dostler (3 February 1892 - 21 August 1917), Pour le Mérite, Royal House Order of Hohenzollern, Military Order of Max Joseph, Iron Cross, a fighter ace credited with 26 victories. His final victory, when he was with Jagdgeschwader I, was scored on 18 August 1917. Three days later, Dostler attacked an R.F.C. R.E.8 of No. 7 Squadron and was hit with machine gun fire. Dostler's aeroplane caught fire and exploded in mid-air. The flaming wreckage fell near Frenzenburg, Belgium.

Herman Goring

Herman Goring 1918 with Fokker D.VII and Richthofen's walking stick

Goring x just after he had taken control of Richthofen's squadron

Fokker Triplane in the background as Goring briefs the fighter pilots

Herman Goring with Fokker DVII

Marine Lt. Carl Kuring of Marine Feld Jasta III in his Pfalz D.IIIa 5940/17.Post – war Kuring was the test pilot of the all-metal Zeppelin Staaken

Ernst Udet (1896-1941) was a German fighter ace who achieved 62 victories during the World War. Udet entered the German Army in 1914 before becoming a fighter pilot with eventual command of 11th Fighter Squadron. He received his pilot training at Darmstadt. It was Udet and his observer Leutnant Bruno Justinus who followed Roland Garros to the ground leading to the capture of Garros, the Morane and the gun interrupter device. Udet fought in Jastas 15, 37, 11 and 4 in amassing his final tally of 62 'kills'. Ultimately forced to retire from active combat in late September 1918 on account of injuries sustained during action: he was (among the Germans) second only to Manfred von Richthofen - the Red Baron - during wartime in terms of his success. Unlike Richthofen however Udet survived the war but not before becoming one of the first fighter pilots to successfully use an escape parachute in action. After the war he married Eleonore "Lo" Zink, he often marked his aircraft with her name, "Lo."

Udet with a Fokker D.VII

Udet in front of an Albatross D.III.

L to R Pfalzer, Weingartner, Udet and Clinkermann with Fokker Eindecker

Unteroffizier Udet (L) Udet with Pour le Merite and 56 kills. In car at steering wheel (2) with Oberlt. Loewenhardt marked 1.

Leutnant Karl Allmenröder (3 May 1896 – 27 June 1917) a flying ace credited with 30 aerial victories. A former medical student, served in the trenches as an 18-year-old artilleryman in the early days of the World War, earning promotion via a battlefield commission to Leutnant on 30 March 1915. After transferring to aviation and serving some time as an artillery spotter in two-seater reconnaissance aeroplanes, he transferred to flying fighter aircraft with Jagdstaffel 11 in November 1916. As Manfred von Richthofen's protégé, Karl Allmenröder scored the first of his 30 confirmed victories on 16 February 1917. Flying a scarlet Albatros D.III (above) trimmed out with white nose and elevators, Allmenröder would score a constant string of aerial victories until 26 June 1917, the day before his death. On 27 June 1917, Karl Allmenröder fell to his death near Zillebeke, Belgium.

Leutnant Emil Koch served with served with Jasta 12 and 32.In 1917 flew a Roland D.VIA of Jasta 32b and was wounded in action 24 October 1918.On 28 May 1918, while flying a Fokker Triplane he shot down an SE5a.Then on 29 August 1918 scored his 7th victory(and last) as CO of Jasta 32 in a Pfalz D.XII and brought down at 09.40, one Sopwith Camel over Aniche

Captain Engelhardt at St Moritz

Captain Paul Engelhardt

In early 1910 Captain Paul Engelhardt and his Wright aeroplane had stopped flying at Johannisthal due to an earlier accident in December 1909. Later as members of the German Wright School, Captain Engelhardt and his mechanic Keidel became two instructors at the Wright School and had a dozen students at the airfield. The German Wright Company included in its directors the Krupps, Rathenaus and other German financier as its backers. Engelhardt was one of the first German pilots to gain a pilot's licence. On 15 March 1910 he flew at St Moritz, to a height of 1800 metres. On 13 May 1910 Engelhardt, with Wright biplane, at Berlin, flew for a period 2 hours 21 minutes and 45 seconds. He was killed in an air crash at Johannisthal on 29th September 1911. He was flying the Wright machine with a passenger, Herr Sedlmayr, a youth of 19, in a fairly strong breeze. Finding the gusts too strong close to the ground, he took the machine up to a height of about 90 feet, when after they had been in the air for an hour and five minutes one of the propellers either burst or became detached and the machine swung round sideways and dived. Captain Engelhardt was picked up dead, and Sedlmayr was severely injured. Captain Engelhardt had jumped clear as the machine struck the ground, this being his custom whenever involved in an accident. In this case, he misjudged his distance and was said to have been struck by the engine. Sedlmayr was later reported as being little hurt. Captain Engelhardt was one of the first three German pilots. Before devoting himself to aviation, he was aide-de-camp to the eldest son of the Kaiser, Crown Prince Wilhelm. He was the first German who ever flew in an aeroplane and had received his instructions from Orville Wright. (Translated/Aeroplane October1911)

Manfred Freiherr Von Richthofen with possibly Udet, behind them a Fokker Triplane of Jasta 11.

Flying officers attached to Rittmeister Manfred Freiherr Von Richthofen's squadron, Jasta 11. Richthofen himself is seated in the Albatros D.III aircraft. From left to right: standing: unidentified (possibly Leutnant Karl Allmenroeder); Hans Hintsch; Vizfeldwebel Sebastian Festner; Leutnant Karl Emil Schaefer; Oberleutnant Kurt Wolff; Georg Simon; Leutnant Otto Brauneck. Sitting: Esser; Krefft; Leutnant Lothar von Richthofen, younger brother of Manfred. 23 April 1917

Paul Schwandt acquired his German Pilot's License No. 85 at Hans Grade's flying school on 20 May 1911. With the help of his father, he acquired his own aircraft to open his own flying school which failed. During the war, Schwandt served as a pilot and flight instructor. Then he became training manager and chief pilot at AEG in Nieder Neuendorf and trained there for the field pilot exam. He crashed an AEG aircraft on delivery to Sweden. During May 1920, Schwandt flew those entitled to vote to Elbing. On the return flight to Stolp, his plane was probably shot down by the Polish military and he lost his life.

Richthofen, seated, with a pyramid of the Emperor's pilots

Oberleutnant Erich Loewenhardt wearing his Pour le Mérite, Iron Cross First Class and Prussian Pilot's Badge. Loewenhardt joined the Imperial German Air Service in 1916. After serving as an aerial observer and reconnaissance pilot, he underwent advanced training to become a fighter pilot with Jagdstaffel 10 in March 1917. Between 24 March 1917 and 10 August 1918, Loewenhardt shot down 45 enemy airplanes, as well as destroying nine observation balloons. Shortly after his final victory, he was killed in a collision with another German pilot.

A gathering of eagles, Oswald Boelcke left of central figure, Max Immelmann to the right of central figure

Aviators from Jasta Boelcke (formerly Jasta 2).In the middle is the squadron leader, Carl Bolle.
To his left is 33 victory ace Ltn. Hermann Frommherz.

Oswald Boelcke started his war career as a pilot in September, 1914 on the Western Front but his first victory did not come until 4 July 1915. When he had sent his seventh victim to his death he was awarded the highest German decoration the Pour le Merite. On 28 October 1916 he was leading the first six of a flight of 12 German machines in an attack on two British 'planes and in diving to the attack he came into collision with one of his comrade's machines. Boelcke could not regain control and down he went in a spin and crashed. He was only 25 when death claimed him. So highly did the British air fighters regard him that a wreath was dropped over the German lines by the Royal Flying Corps, with a card inscribed, "To the memory of Captain Boelcke, our brave and chivalrous opponent."

Friedrich Christiansen and Hansa-Brandenburg W.12 seaplane

In August 1914, Friedrich Christiansen was conscripted and posted to Zeebrugge as a naval aviator. He flew Hansa-Brandenburg W.12 seaplanes over the North Sea, the English Channel, and Great Britain. For his bombing missions on Dover and Ramsgate, he was awarded the Iron Cross 2nd Class. From 1915 to 1916 Christiansen went on numerous reconnaissance and bombing missions, helping to make his unit at Zeebrugge one of the most successful in the German Naval Air Service. On 27 April 1916, as Leutnant der Matrosen Artillerie (Lieutenant of Naval Artillery,) Christiansen was awarded the Iron Cross 1st Class and Knights Cross with Swords of the House Order of Hohenzollern.By December 1917 he was awarded the Pour le Mérite ("Blue Max"), the first of only three given to naval aviators and the only one to a seaplane pilot.). By 11 November 1918 he raised his personal tally to 13, as well as some shared victories, which cumulatively may have brought his total to 21.

Oberleutnant Henrich Claudius Kroll (3 November 1894 – 21 February 1930) Pour le Merite, Knight's Cross of the Royal House Order of Hohenzollern, Saxony's Albert Order Knight Second Class with Swords, Iron Cross First and Second Class, fighter ace credited with 33 victories. Appointed commanding officer of Royal Saxon Jasta 24 on 1 July 1917. He flew a Pfalz fighter and on 25 May 1918, his Jasta finally received Fokker D.VIIs. Only four of Kroll's victims had been two-seater reconnaissance aircraft. Kroll shot down about as many enemy fighters as his more famous compatriot, Manfred von Richthofen.

Oberleutnant Friedrich Ritter von Röth (29 September 1893 – 31 December 1918) was a fighter ace with 28 victories. He was the most successful German pilot at the extremely hazardous practice of shooting down observation balloons and destroyed 20 of them. A Fokker D.VII pilot he scored ten victories with this type of aircraft. Röth was awarded Germany's highest decoration for valour, the Pour le Mérite, on 8 September 1918.Distressed by his nation's loss of the war, and by his religious convictions against killing, he shot himself on 31 December 1918 and on death was raised to Ritter, which gave him a posthumous knighthood.

Vizefeldwebel Friedrich Manschott (21 February 1893 – 16 March 1917) was a flying ace credited with 12 aerial victories. On the day of his death, on 16 March 1917, he destroyed an enemy captive balloon but was brought down in combat with four Caudrons. In three months he had defeated eleven opponents, eight in flight and three captive balloons. Friedrich Manschott was born on 21 February 1893. Before the war he was a recruit in the First Baden infantry Regiment; at the beginning of the war, August 1914 he became a motorcyclist and then at the start of 1915 he became a flight instructor by 10 August 1916 he had received his instructors certificate. He was then transferred to a fighter unit, Jagdstaffel 7 between 5 January and 16 March 1917 flying Albatros fighters. He had been promoted to sergeant on 17 November 1916 because of his courage.

Heinrich Bongartz (31 January 1892 – 23 January 1946), fighter pilot ace credited with 33 confirmed victories and one unconfirmed. On 23 December 1917, he was personally awarded the Pour le Mérite by Kaiser Wilhelm II. Units served Flieger-Abteilung 5; Jagdstaffel 36, Kampfstaffel 27 and flew Fokker Triplanes.

Hauptmann Rudolf Kleine (26 August 1886 to 12 December 1917)On 4 October 1917 Kleine was awarded the Pour le Mérite for outstanding leadership, distinguished military planning and the successful operations carried out by Kagohl 3. The award was given in particular recognition to his leading six raids on London between 24 September and 2 October, as well as organizing raids against Harwich, Dover, Chatham and Sheerness and the French city of Calais. Unfortunately, on 12 December 1917 he was intercepted by a flight of Nieuport 27's. Kleine's plane was shot down by Capt. WW Rogers of No 1 Sqdn RFC. The plane first caught fire, then fell to pieces and crashed.

Bruno Loerzer (22 January 1891 – 23 August 1960) was credited with 44 aerial victories during World War I, he was a commander of one of the first Imperial German Air Service Jagdeschwaders His tally reached 20 victories at the end of October 1917 and he received the Pour le Mérite in February 1918.That same month, he took command of the newly formed Jagdgeschwader III, the third of Germany's famed "flying circuses."

Werner Voss (13 April 1897 – 23 September 1917) credited with 48 aerial victories. He began his military career in November 1914 as a 17-year-old Hussar. After turning to aviation, he proved to be a natural pilot. After flight school and six months in a bomber unit, he joined a newly formed fighter squadron, Jagdstaffel 2 on 21 November 1916. By 6 April 1917, Voss had scored 24 victories and had been awarded Germany's highest award, the Pour le Mérite. On 23 September 1917 Voss battled with McCudden, of No. 56 Squadron (S.E.5a) who was in the fight with a flight of his squadron. Voss, who was in a red nosed Fokker triplane, fought seven British machines single-handed for some ten minutes with magnificent courage and skill and was finally killed by Sec.Lt. A. P. F. Rhys-Davids, of No. 56 Squadron.

Fokker Triplane ascribed to Werner Voss

Leutnant Hartmuth Baldamus (10 August 1891 – 14 April 1917) flying ace credited with 18 aerial victories. He flew a two-seater reconnaissance aircraft for Feldflieger Abteilung 20, beginning 29 March 1915. Posted to fly fighters with Jagdstaffel 5 and moved on to Jagdstaffel 9 in early November 1916. His score reached 17 by 12 April 1917. He lost his life in a collision with a French Nieuport 14 April 1917.

Oberleutnant Hans Berr (20 May 1890–6 April 1917) He helped pioneer the world's first dedicated fighteraeroplane, the Fokker Eindekker "flying gun". Berr took command of one of the world's original fighter squadrons, Jagdstaffel 5.He was awarded Germany's highest military honour, the Pour le Merite, on 4 December 1916.On Good Friday, 6 April 1917, Berr and his wingman Paul Hoppe collided and were killed while engaged in a dogfight with RFC fighters.

Wilhelm Frankl (20 December 1893 – 8 April 1917), Pour le Mérite, Royal House Order of Hohenzollern, Iron Cross, was a World War I fighter ace credited with 20 aerial victories. He scored his first aerial victory with a carbine on 10 May 1915.In late December 1916 Frankl took command of Jasta 4. Frankl's end came on 8 April 1917. While battling Bristol F.2 Fighters of No. 48 Squadron RFC, his Albatros D.III lost its lower wing under combat manoeuvres and he and his collapsed aircraft fell 2600 ft.

Karl Emil Schäfer (17 December 1891 – 5 June 1917) became one of the major German flying aces of the war, with 30 confirmed aerial victories. As a pilot he served on the Eastern Front with Kampfgeschwader 2 from July 1916 onwards, he moved to the west and flew with Kampfstaffel 11 of KG 2. Schäfer was then given command of Jasta 28 on 26 April 1917 and gained further victories for a total of 30 claims. Schäfer was shot down and killed on 5 June 1917 in combat. With 29 of his victories flying the Albatros D.III, he was one of the most successful pilots on the type.

Ernst von Hoeppner *General der Kavallerie*

From the autumn of 1916, when Hoeppner was entrusted with the newly created post of Commander General of the Air Force, General von Hoeppner was responsible for the building of the re-organised German air arm. Ernst von Hoeppner was born on 14 June 1860 in Tonnin on the Pomeranian island of Wollin. From the training depot he became a second lieutenant to the Dragoon Regiment No. 6 in Stendal. After a temporary assignment to the War Academy, he was transferred in 1893 as a squadron chief to the Dragoon Regiment No. II in Colmar im Elsali. Appointed to the General Staff in 1902, he was from 1904 as 1st General Staff Officer in the 9th Army Corps in Altona. In 1906 Lieutenant Colonel von Hoeppner became commander of Hussar Regiment No. 13 in Diedenhofen. then from August 1908. Chief of Staff of the 7th Army Corps. In September 1912 he was appointed commander of the 4th Cavalry Brigade in Bromberg. In 1913 he was raised to the German hereditary peerage. At the beginning of the Great War, Hoeppner became Chief of Staff of the 3rd Army. He held this responsible office to the spring of 1915, when he was given command of the 14th Reserve Division of the First Army. In 1915 Hoeppner became Chief of the General Staff of the 2nd Army and then in 1916 commander of the 75th Reserve Division, which at that time stood at Lake Narocz in the defensive fight against numbers of superior Russian army units. In the midst of heavy fighting, Hoeppner was appointed Commanding General of the Air Force, a post he held until the end of World War I. His great services to the development of the German Air Force were particularly recognized on 8 April 1917 by the award of the Order Pour le Merite. - Ernst von Hoeppner spent the last years of his life on his estate Gross-Mokraz on the island of WoIlin. There he was transferred to the Reserve Army on 25 September 1922. On 26 September 1922 Hoeppner died of Influenza at the age of 62. He was buried in his birthplace, Tonnin, on the island of Wollin. (Translated)

Herman von der Lieth Thomsen

Hermann von der Lieth-Thorasen was born on 10 March 1867 in Jensburg, and came from a long-established Dithmarschern family. He joined the Army in 1887 and was promoted to lieutenant in 1889. After graduating from the War Academy, Thomsen was transferred to the General Staff, where he remained until the beginning of 1914. In the spring of 1914 he was appointed General Staff Officer at the Inspection of Aviation and Motor Navigation. Thomsen took part in the Battle of Tannenberg and was assigned to the General Command of Reserve Corps 24 in September 1914 as 1st General Staff Officer. He fought at Ypres and took part in the winter campaign in the Carpathians. When the expansion of the air force became increasingly necessary, Lieutenant Colonel Thomsen was appointed in March 1915 as "Chief of Field Air Forces" in General Headquarters and assigned to the Supreme Army Command. In the autumn of 1916 he was appointed Chief of the General Staff of the Commanding General of the Air Force. This was his greatest work together with Lieutenant General Hoeppner and his organisation skills in this post were rewarded on 8 April 1917 by the award of the Pour le Merite. Thomsen, promoted to Oberst, remained in this important post until the Armistice. He then directed the demobilization demanded by the Versailles Treaty and headed for a short time in the then Air Force department in the Prussian War Ministry. Then he retired from military service in August 1919 with the rank of colonel. He rejoined the reformed Luftwaffe under Herman Goering in 1935. Hermann von der Lieth-Thomsen died on 5 May 1942 whilst in service as General de Flieger in Sylt and was buried in the Invalidenfriedhof Cemetery in Berlin. (Translated)

Hans-Joachim Buddecke (22 August 1890 – 10 March 1918) flying ace credited with thirteen victories. He was the third ace, after Max Immelmann and Oswald Boelcke, to earn the Blue Max (Pour le Mérite). He saw combat in three combat theatres, Turkey, and the Western Front. Buddecke was killed during an aerial combat above Lens, France on 10 March 1918, victim to Sopwith Camels of 3 Naval Squadron RNAS. Hans-Joachim Buddecke is buried at the Invalidenfriedhof Cemetery in Berlin.

Karl Bolle (20 June 1893 – 9 October 1955), was a fighter ace with 36 aerial victories. He became a Jagdstaffel commander during the Great War. Promoted to Oberleutnant and transferred to command Jagdstaffel 2 on 20 February 1918 at Marcke, France. This was the squadron that Oswald Boelcke had commanded. It was re-equipped with Fokker Dr.I triplanes as it was being incorporated into Jagdgeschwader 3. At the time of the Armistice he surrendered his squadron of Fokker D.VIIs to the British at Nivelles France

Vizefeldwebel Sebastian Festner (30 June 1894 – 25 April 1917) He was credited with 12 victories. He was a mechanic with Flieger Abtleilung Nr. 1 in October 1914. Posted to Flieger Abtleilung Nr. 7b in February 1915 as a Gefreiter, Festner learned to fly unofficially and then underwent training with Flieger-ersatz-Abteilung 2b and Fliegerersatz-Abteilung 5b.He was then posted to Jagdstaffel 11, then under the command of Manfred von Richthofen, on 10 November 1916.Flying an Albatros D.III, Festner was killed in action on 25 April 1917, near Oppy..

Leutnant Hartmuth Baldamus in the cockpit of his fighter

Leutnant Karl Menckhoff of Jasta 3 and later Jasta 72

Leutnant Dannhubbe

Flieger Hauptman Hans Hesse (21.05.1865 - 08.11.1938) He was awarded the Order pour le Mérite on 11.12.1916 while serving as Chef d.Gen. St. d. 9. Armee (full dates 08.09.16 - 09.04.17). He served in Turkey and was active in politics in Berlin during the revolution; he was credited with 34 kills.

Leutnants Hans Horn and Johnke

Haptmann A. Keller

Leutnant Kissenberth

Leutnant Max Muller

Eduard v. Schleich

Melli Beese

Germany's first women pilot brevet 115 (13-Sept.-1911)

Amelie Hedwig Beese was born in Dresden on 13 September 1886 to Alma Wilhemine Hedwig Beese and Friedrich Karl Richard Beese, an architect and stone artist. She had a younger brother Edgar and two half siblings from her father's first marriage, Hertha and Kurt. The family were comfortably well off. In 1906 Beese decided to pursue a career as a sculptor; however, she had to leave her native Germany to study, as German art schools did not admit female students. She studied instead at Stockholm's Royal Academy from 1906 until 1909 and created a number of works including a bronze bust of the painter Allan Egnell which has survived. She won a prize for a group sculpture, The Soccer Player. Melli Beese was taught to fly on a Wright at the "Ad Astra" school.

She earned her license on 13 September 1911 and the following day broke Helen Dutrieu's altitude record. After finally getting her license, Melli set a succession of endurance and altitude records and later studied under Helmuth Hirth,learning to fly a monoplane. She built her own aircraft, the "Melli Beese Colombe" (Melli Beese's Dove [or pigeon]), which she used in her flight school. It seems to have been a Taube modification, in which she later reportedly made the amazing speed of 120 kilometers per hour. Interestingly, she is one of the first of several women pilots who opened their own flight schools (hers started in early 1912 opened at Johannisthal, Berlin.) The school opened in partnership with Frenchman Charles Boutard and Hermann Reichelt. (Charles Boutard was born in Paris8 Juillet 1884.) Boutard had completed his apprenticeship as a mechanic at the Poulin aircraft company in Johannisthal and also got his pilot's license there on4 April 1912. He had also served as a second lieutenant in French colonial infantry. They bought three planes and Adolph Ludwig joined them as the school's mechanic. Boutard gained a German flying license on 4 April 1912 and helped Melli with teaching her pupils to fly.

The school had a good safety record but wasn't able to attract enough pupils, so Beese had to let Reichelt go. She was one of the few to make her school prosper, keeping it running till April 1914. The chief pilot at her flying school was the Frenchman Charles Boutard, whom she was to marry in January 1913. She was granted at least two aviation patents; one was for a hydroplane (seaplane). She established a factory to produce these hydroplanes (or at least to finish airframes produced by another company). The war ruined her plans, as she and her French husband were considered enemy aliens and interned initially in Hollzminden. The couple was placed under house arrest in Wittstock an der Dosse in 1917, as Charles Boutard was now considered an enemy alien as was she. Boutard was in and out of prison and Melli Beese was prevented from flying, teaching, or building aircraft. After the war, they returned to aviation and tried to plan a round-the-world flight in 1921, for which they were unable to find sponsors.

They sued the German government for compensation but inflation ruined any settlement. Melli and Boutard were divorced in the early 20s and he ended up driving taxi cabs in Berlin. She shot herself on 22 December 1925 in her Berlin flat and is buried in the cemetery at Berlin-Schmargendorf, Boutard earned his living as a chauffeur until 1935. Charles Boutard passed away in Berlin – Buch 26 January 1952.

Melli Beese is quoted in several publications as having a motto, "Flying is everything; living is nothing."

Amelie Hedwig Beese and with her husband Charles Boutard 1913

Offizier Stellvertreter Rudolf Klimke

Albatross C.VII used by Feld Flieger Abteilung 55 used to bomb London 6/7 May 1917

Rudolf Klimke was transferred to Flieger-Abteilung 19 (Flier Detachment 19) which provided reconnaissance for the German 4 Army in Flanders. Klimke had taught himself night flying. On the night of 6/7 May 1917, Klimke and aerial observer Oberleutnant Walter Leon flew an Albatros C.VII out of an airfield near Ostend, Belgium. The commander of Flieger-Abteilung 19 (Flier Detachment 19), Hauptman Baer, had authorized their bombing of England. When Klimke and Leon returned to Handzaeme after dropping five ten-kilogram bombs on Hackney and Holloway, they were reprimanded. Later the group was inspected by General von Hoeppner and Klimke and Leon were presented to the General as the London bombers. Nevertheless, Klimke would raid England again, on 7 July 1917. Flying a three-seater Gotha for Kampfgeschwader 3 (Tactical Bomber Wing 3), he shot down a Sopwith over London for his second aerial victory.

Later, Leon was promoted to commanding officer of Flieger Abteilung 19. Klimke finished the war as a fighter pilot in Jagdstaffel 27 flying the Fokker D.VII. It is not known what model fighter he was flying on 21 September 1918, when he shot down a Sopwith Camel for his 17th victim. It is known that the crew of a Bristol F.2b hit Klimke in the shoulder with three bullets. Somehow he managed to fly back to the safety of his home field and land. He was rushed from the airfield to the hospital. The hospital was bombed that night. The war ended before Klimke could heal enough to return to flying duties. He had been awarded the Iron Cross First Class and he was officially credited with 16 victories.

Members of the German Air Force who were awarded the Pour le Merite

Oswald Boelcke
Max Immelmann
Manfred Frhr. v. Richthofen
Hermann Goring
Ernst Udet
Ernst v. Hoeppner
Hermann v. d. Lieth-Thomsen
Karl Ailmenroeder
Oliver Frhr. v. Beaulieu-Marconnay
Paul Baumer
Otto Bernerr
Hans Berr
Rudolf Berthold
Walter Blume
Erwin Bohme
Oskar Frhr. v. Boenigk
Carl Bolle
Heinrich Bongartz
Ernst Brandenburg
Julius Buckler
Hans-Joachim Buddecke
Franz Buchner
Walter v. Bulow
Friedrich Christiansen
Karl Degclow
Albert Dossenbach
Eduard Ritter v. Dostler
Hermann Fricke
Heinrich Gontermann
Robert Ritter v. Greim
Wilhelm Griebsch
Jurgen v. Grone
Walter Hohndorf
Erich Homburg
Hans-Georg Horn
Joseph Jacobs
Alfred Keller
Hans Kirschstein
Otto Kissenberth
Hans Klein
Rudolf Kleine
Hermann Kohl
Otto Konnecke
Heinrich Kroll
Arthur Laumann
Gustav Leffers
Leo Leonhardy
Erich Loewenhardt
Bruno Loerzer
Max Ritter v. Muller
Albert Muller-Kahle
Max Ritter v. Mulzer
Ulrich Neckel
Friedrich Nielebock
Theodor Osterkamp
Otto Parschau
Paul Frhr. v. Pechmann
Fritz Putter
Lothar Frhr. v. Richthofen
Peter Rieper
Fritz Ritter v. Roth
Fritz Rumey
Gotthard Sachsenberg
Karl-Emil Schafer
Eduard Ritter v. Schleith
Peter Strasser
Karl Thom
Emil Thuy
Horst Treusch v. Buttlar-Brandenfels
Adolf Ritter v. Tutschek
Josef Veltjens
Werner Voss
Franz Walz
Rudolf Windisch
Kurt Wintgens
Kurt Wolff
Kurt Wusthoff

INSTRUCTION AND TRAINING OF AVIATORS

The training of pilots was usually done in Germany. It began in an Aviation school, usually a civil school or one of the many schools created by aeroplane manufacturers and continued with a training or Reserve unit (Flieger-ersatzabeilungen). An idea of the examination given to obtain a flying certificate (brevet) can be got from the interrogation of German prisoners. According to one aviator captured in May 1918 the examinations were:-

1. First examination conferring the title of Pilots:-
   a. To fly and make six figures of eight.
   b. Land in a circle 50 metres in diameter.
   c. Fifteen landings.
2. Second examination conferring the title of Field-Pilot (Feld-Pilote)
   a. Flight of half an hour, at an altitude of 3000 metres with a spiral landing.
   b. A flight of one hour at 3000 metres.
   c. Landing in a circle of 60 metres in diameter, from a height of 500 metres.
3. Third examination conferring the title of Flugmeister on the Pilot.
   a. 10 landings in a space of 100 metres wide, from a height of 800 metres.
   b. Same thing front a height of 1000 metres, without power, motor stopped.
   c. Ten landings in a space 100 metres wide, from a height of 2000 metres.
   d. Same thing from a height of 4000 metres, with engine stopped.
   e. Flight of 120 Kilometres, across country an return over a prescribed route.

Earlier a German aviator captured in July 1917 explained how there were four examinations. The first two examinations were made in a civil school and the last two with a depot squadron.

1. First Examinations:-
   a. Two flights making six figure of eights and landing in a circle with a radius of 25 metres.

Albatros C.1 used as a trainer

L.V.G. B1

NFW B.I at Johannisthal

2. Second Examinations:-
    a. Five landings from a height of 500 metres, the signal to land being given by a pistol shot,
    b. Ten landings from a height of 800 metres, in a circle with a 25 meter radius.
    c. Ten landings in a circle within a 25 metres radius from a height of 1000 metres, engine stopped,
    d. Flight of one hour, at a height of more than 2500 metres.

These examinations were given in an 80 to 100 h.p. aeroplane.

3. Third Examinations:-
    a. Five landings from a signal given by a pistol shot.
    b. Five landings from a height of 800 metres.
    c. Five landings from a height of 1000 metres.
    d. Five landings in unknown country.
    e. Two flights of 100 kilometres, with an Observer.
    f. Four successive trials in aerial combat.
    g. Four successive trials in aerial combat at a height of 2000 metres or more, including the taking of photographs.
    h. Flight of 250 kilometres, with an Observer landing during the trip.

These examinations were given in 120 to 150 h.p. Machines.

4. Fourth Examinations:-

Flights in different, new high powered, one-seater and two-seater machines, machine gun firing during the flight.

The training of pilots lasted generally from five to six months.

Scout (Fighter) Pilots were selected from the pilots at the front. They receive a special instruction in a scout school.

Rumpler C.1

OBSERVERS

Observers received their training probably at the Aviation Training Depots, or as was more frequently the case at Aviation Parks in the North of France. Their instruction consisted of lectures on tactical and technical subjects and practical exercises. Lectures were given on German and Entente aviation, wireless telegraphy, artillery ranging, photography, the meteorological service and the making of reports. Practical exercises consist of flight with or without a tactical mission: machine gun firing at a ground target, aerial combat lasting not less than 15 minutes, during which the observer took photographs of his opponent. The course finished with three examinations.

The first examination was on the writing of a report. The second was on various reconnaissance works and ranging. The third was on photographic reconnaissance and machine gun fitting. The duration of the training course was about two months.

A report by Lieutenant Baldamus of Artillery Flight 201, German Air Service, on the conditions permitting a man to have the brevet (wings) and insignia of Observer were:-

a. 25 flights over the Entente lines.
b. Taking of 25 photographs.
c. One Aerial fight.
d. Two night flights.
e. Two bomb dropping flights.
f. Receive by wireless telegraphy 60 letters in a minute and send in 40 letters a minute.

More time was spent in the training of Observers than in that of Pilots. At Hanover there was a preparatory school for Observers. The average duration of the course being six weeks and on completion of the course the pupils were sent to a regular Observers' School for a course of instruction of three months. An Observation School accommodating 50 pupils was located at Thorn (East Prussia) and had been established at Cologne. On completion of the 4 ½ months instruction, Observers were drafted to Army Aircraft Parks in the same way as pilots and thence allotted to Units at the Front.

(Note: - translated from sur l'Aviation Allemande and a paper on German Air Service communicated by the Aviation Section of the French Military Mission.)

Rumpler C.VIII

FLIEGER-ERSATZ-ABTEILUNG

Approximately 150 to 180 recruits were drawn from civilian employment for each Flieger-Ersatz-Abteilung every three months, preference being given to experienced workmen such as locksmiths, mechanics, turners, etc. In addition, men with technical knowledge from other branches of the Army, who are no longer fit for active service, were drafted into the Flieger-Ersatz-Abteilungen. These far outnumbered the civilians, it was, however impossible to give exact figures in the latter case.

Flying personnel were drawn from the above mentioned sources as well as from officers and men who had volunteered for the Air Service. Since volunteers were very numerous, it was possible to maintain a high physical standard. The medical examination was very strict but apparatus for nerve testing was not used.

PRELIMINARY SCHOOL TRAINING

FLYING PERSONNEL

Pilots were trained in the Flieger-Ersatz-Abteilung (a) and the tached Militar Flieger Schulen. (Military Flying Schools).

VORRATSSCHULE

Pupils joining the Flieger-Ersatz Abteilungen from other branches of the Army immediately enter the Vorratsschule, while civilians were first trained in the Rekrutenkompagnie, (recruit company). The course comprised lectures on engine construction, meteorology, the compass and map-reading. Elementary practical instruction in assembling and dismantling of airplanes was given by mechanics under the supervision of a Werkmeister (Equipment Officer). The lecturers were all officers and NCOs. The pupils stayed at this school on an average from 4 to 12 weeks, according to the number of vacancies at the flying school. Owing to the larger number of flying pupils a Vorratsschule was attached to several Beobachterschulent (Observers School) and Flieger Funker Schule (Wireless School). After passing an easy examination on the termination of his course at the Vorratsschule, the pupil entered either Fliegerkompagnie der Flieger-Ersatz-Abteilung or was sent to the attached Militar Flieger Schule.

MILITAR FLIEGAR SCHULE (Military Flying School)

These schools were conducted by private firms; the training program was proscribed by the Inspektion der Flieger-turppen (High Command of the Air Service). An officer in charge of the school represented the interests of the Flieg.-T was responsible for the running of the school strictly on the lines laid down by the High Command. Flying Instruction was under the control of the Chief Pilot employed by the firm. The efforts of each firm to obtain first-class instructors and lecturers promoted competition between the firms, which had a considerable influence on the efficiency of the schools. For a fee of 8000 marks the firms undertook to provide machines, instructors and free board and lodging of the pupils up to the second examination. It was obvious, therefore, that the company had a financial interest in preparing the pilots for the second examination in as short a time as possible. In the case of pupils who failed to pass the second examination the State payed 50 marks for each flight up to a maximum of 3500 marks. While a majority of pupils were officers, a large number of other ranks are also trained at Militar Flieger Schulen.

Each instructor had 6 to 10 pupils, whom he trained on two dual control machines and at least 4 machines for solo flight. By the spring of 1918 the number of flights on dual control machines had been cut down to 30. Civilian flying instructors received a minimum pay of 300 Marks per month, plus a premium of 250 to 350 Marks for every pupil who passed the second examination, a large part of which premium was paid after the pupil had passed the first examination. It was no longer customary to make deductions from the instructor's premium each time a pupil crashed.

FLYING PAY

Flying Pay of 150 marks per month was given to pupils dating from their first flight.

FLIEGERKOMPAGNE DER FLIEGER-ERSATZ ABTEILUNG

Those Vorratsschuler who were not sent to a Militar Flieger Schule received their practical and theoretical training at the Flieger-kompagnie der Flieger-Ersatz-Abteilung, where the whole of the course was in the hands of military instructors. Flying instructors were always N.C.O.'s. Owing to the nonexistence of the premium and to the fact that private influence played an important part in the selection of candidates for those posts, the instructing staff of a Flieger kompagnie was usually greatly inferior to that of a Militar Flieger Schule. Up to the second examination N.C.O.'s and men formed the majority of pupils at the Flieger-Ersatz-Abteilungen. Although each instructor had only five to eight pupils allotted to him, he took almost double the time in training them that the civilian instructor at Militar Flieger Schule took. With very few exceptions the third examination has to be passed by pilots at a Flieger-Ersatz-Abteilung. The only correction regarding the tests of the third examination was that the five landings out-side the aerodrome were made from a height of only 500 metres. By the summer of 1918 there was no shortage of school machines at the Flieger-Ersatz-Abteilungen due to the large number of C machines returned from the front which no longer satisfied the requirements of the fighting units. The considerable material at the Russian and Rumanian front, consisted mostly of more or less obsolete C machines which had also been sent to the Flieger-Ersatz-Abteilungen.

FLUG PARK (Air Parks)

As a rule pilots were sent to the Parks only after having passed the third examination but in order to relieve the pressure at the Flieger-Ersatz-Abteilungen, pilots were sometimes allowed to pass some of the tests of the third examination at the Park. The first four tests, however, had to be passed at the Flieger-Ersatz-Abteilung. The Pilots who had finished their training remained one to three months at the Park where they practiced flying on the latest type machines.

NUMBER OF PUPILS WHO DO NOT BECOME FLYING PERSONNEL AT THE FRONT

Fliegerkompagnie: Average number of pupils in 1918 about 250. About 100 Vorratsschuler, permanent staff of about 60 mechanics.
Werftkompagnie: Permanent Staff of about 250 air mechanics. Approximately 30 mechanics (Werftschuler) were trained per month.
Ersatskompagnle: On an average 400 air mechanics; guard and orderlies.
Rekrutenkompignie: On an average 150 men remained in this company for three months for discipline and general military training, these men were drafted into any of the three companies mentioned above, as required.
Apart from these companies Beobachter Zuge (observation courses) and in some cases Flieger Schutzen Zuge (gunnery courses) was attached to Flieger-Ersatz-Abteilungen.

SPECIAL TRAINING OF PILOTS

Suitable pilots were selected for special training on single seaters and twin engine machines after completion of their course on two-seaters. The former were trained as scout pilots at the Flieger-Ersatz-Abteilung; pilots who had flown at the front and wished to become scout pilots were sent to a Jagdstaffelschule (Pursuit Flight School). Pilots, of G machines were trained at the Geschwaderschule (Squadron School) where formation flying was practiced to a very great extent. Pilots of R machines are sent to the Riesen-Ersatz-Abteilung (Giant aeroplane training section). As a rule only pilots who have flown at the front are sent here.

BEOBACHTER SCHULE (Observer's School)

After a stay of four weeks at the Beobachter Zuge (observation course) of a Flieger-Ersatz-Abteilungithe observer pupil was sent to a Beobachter Schule (observer's school) or an Artillerie Fliege Schule (artillery observation school). The length of the course was approximately eight weeks.

Flieger Schutzen Zug (Machine Gunners Course) Apart from the Flieger Schutzen Zuge at some Flieger-Ersatz-Abteilungen and Observers' Schools, no schools for machine gunner were known to exist. The training was similar to that carried out at observers' schools, as many machine gunners who had passed the Ein-jahrige (one year) were afterwards given commissions as observers. In addition to the ordinary observers' course a very thorough training was given in machine gunnery and aerial fighting. *

**This translation is not clear Ed.*

Gunnery training is carried out as follows:

1) Target practice.
2) Firing on the ground behind a revolving propeller.
3) Firing from a machine at targets on the ground.

Firing at targets from fast motor cars was also practised. The whole course lasted from eight to ten weeks.

FLIEGER FUNKER SCHULE (Wireless Telegraphy School)

Since 1st April 1913, only officer-observers for artillery and long distance bombing flights, as well as wireless telegraphy operators (Bordfunker) for giant machines, were trained. The officers and wireless telegraphy operators went through an advanced course lasting four weeks in all branches of aviation wireless telegraphy work. It should be noted that before joining this school the officers had already gone through a course of eight weeks at an Observer's or Artillerie Flieger Schule and the wireless telegraphy operators had been trained for three to six months at a Nea Signals School. Only wireless telegraphy operators who could send and receive at a minimum speed of 100 letters per minute were sent to a Flieger Funker Schule. On the other hand the speed attained by the officers joining the course at the Flieger Funker Schule was considerably less, owing chiefly to the lack of interest in their work, shown by these gentlemen and the typical mental attitude of the German Officer who thinks that he can do everything and anything without having to work for it like any ordinary human being.

In addition to the pupils mentioned above wireless telegraphy mechanics (F.T. Warte) were also trained at the Flieger Funker Schule. Their duties were to fit wireless telegraphy apparatus on the machines to keep it in order and test it. The wireless telegraphy pupil mechanic took part in a number of flights until he was capable of tuning an apparatus correctly and of getting into communication in the usual way with the wireless telegraphy ground station, (Flughafenstation). The advanced pupil was also trained in communicating with his own station in spite of several interrupter stations working at the same time.

ORGANIZATION OF A FLIEGER FUNKER SCHULE (Neu Ruppin)

Two "Oflas" (Offizers Lehr Abteilungen - Officers' Training Sections) trained on an average 70 officers per month. About 2/3 of these were observer pupils, the rest being trained observers sent back from the front. In addition there were two schools for wireless telegraphy mechanics: one Werft Abteilung Werft with about 150 mechanics and one Flug Abteilung to which the whole of the rest of the permanent staff belonged. Altogether there were about 1000 men at Neu Ruppin in June 1918. A captain was in command, the various Abteilungen were commanded by Lieutenants. There were also permanent staffs of fifteen officers. The buildings at the Flieger Funker Schule consisted of one Werft, six completed and two nearly completed hangars. The hangars were of the standard type used at the new Flieger-Ersatz-Abteilungen and could house twelve machines of the Albatros type C.VII.

TRAINING OF AIR MECHANICS

1. By attaching them to the first class training of auxiliary mechanics.
2. Course at the Werftschule of a Flieger-Ersatz-Abteilung.

3. Course at the works of various motor firms.

At the Werftschulen only a general training was given and there were separate courses lasting as a rule four weeks for special classes of mechanics such as riggers, splicers, and welders. Men who were attached to engine firms received special training in the type manufactured at the works. In spite of the fact that great care was taken to make the course as complete as possible, the present system did not appear to be satisfactory and there was a lack of good mechanics.

RATIONS OF FLYING PERSONNEL AND AIR MECHANICS

At home, as well as at the front, the food of the flying personnel was much better than that of the air mechanics. Extra rations of meat and bread were only issued to the flying men. One of the reasons for the small rations at aerodromes at home was to be found in the fact that the cooks disposed of a part of the food to civilians.

SCHOOL MACHINES (CHIEFLY IN USE AT FLIEGER-ERSATZ-ABTEILUNG)

Albatros type B. and C. I. to XII.
Aviatik " " " 200 h.p. Benz motor.
A.E.G. " " " 180 h.p. Opel-Argus motor.
D. F. W. " " " 200 h.p. Benz motor.
Fokker old two-seater biplane.
Germania type B.
Gotha H " and C.
Halberstadt type B and C to 180 h.p. Mercedes motor
L.V.G. " " " C.L. to 200 h.p. Benz motor.
Merkur " C.
M. F. W. Rumpler Lizenz type C.I.
Roland Walfisch
Rumpler type B and C.L. to 200h.p. BENZ motor.

Pilots who had passed the third examination had the following single seaters at their disposal.

Albatros type D.I. to D. III.
Fokker monoplane and old biplanes D.I. to D.V.
Halberstadt type D 120 h.p. Argus motor.
Pfalz old type
Roland

Roland C.11 Walfisch

Germania B.1

Aviatik B.II

It was considered of great importance that pilots should fly as many types of C machines as possible between the second and third examinations. At Militar Flieger Schulen most of the flying was done on B machines manufactured by the firms. At the Observer's Schools C machines only were in use. Latterly, however, a few single seaters had been put at the disposal of pilots at these schools. Only C and G machines are in use at Geschwaderschulen. At the Riesen-Ersatz-Abteilungen all types of D.C.G. and R machines were in use. At Jagdstaffelschulen the most modern types of D machines were flown.

LIST OF SCHOOLS (FLIEGER-ERSATZ-ABTEILUNGEN)

No

1. Altenburg. S.A.
2. Schneidemühl
3. Gotha.
4. Posen.
5. Hannover.
6. Grossanham.
7. Braunschweig. Transferred from Cologne not yet fully developed. (Nov 1918)
8. Craudenz.
9. Darmstadt.
10. Boblingen
11. Brieg
12. Kottbus Not fully developed
13. Brouberg
14. Halle
15. Konnigsberg

BAVARAN MILITARY FLIEGER SCHULEN

(SAME AS FLIEGER-ERSATZ-ABTEILUNGSN IN THE REST OF GERMANY)

No.

1. Schleissheim
2. Heustadt a.d.h. Not fully developed.
3. Furth - nearly complete.
4. Germersheim- not fully developed.

The following Flieger-Ersatz-Abteilungen were being built at the present time. Five Flieger-Ersatz-Abteilungen on the Muritzee (at Muron, Waren). It was said that this would be the greatest flying centre in Germany. One Flieger-Ersatz-Abteilung at Furstenwalde Weimar, Wurzen i/Sa, Luckenwalde West Saxony, (Chemitz or Zwickau). It was reported that the total number of Flieger-Ersatz-Abteilungen in Germany was to be increased to 48. The opinion prevailing in well informed circles in Germany was that this large number of projected new centres was not the outcome of the immediate needs of the Army but that they were being formed in view of the opposition expected in the Reichstag after the war to increased Army expenditure. In this connection it was interesting to note that the accommodation on the aerodrome of recently organized Flieger-Ersatz-Abteilungen was in excess of the wants of the present establishment in personnel and material.

FLUGSTUTZPUNKTC (LANDING GROUNDS AND SHEDs)

Believed to exist at the following places:
Hamburg Bremen Hagenau Lubeck Wurzbug Bautzen Gersthofen Hundsfeld Osnabruck Zittau

MILITARY FLIEGER SCHULEN

A.E.G. Niederneuendorf Attached to Flieger-Ersatz Abteilung.
Albatros Schneidemuhl Attached to Flieger-Ersatz-Abteilung 2.
Aviatik Bork i/M Attached to Flieger-Ersatz-Abteilung 3.
D. F. W. Leipzig-Mockau Attached to Flieger- Ersatz-Abteilung 6
Leipzig-Lindenthal Attached to Flieger- Ersatz-Abteilung 6
Travemuende Attached to Flieger-Ersatz-Abteilung 6
Gothaer Waggonfabrik Gotha Attached to Flieger- Ersatz -Abteilung 3
Halberstaedter Flugzugwerke Halberstadt Attached to Flieger- Ersatz-Abteilung 5.

Hansa Flugzeugwerke Hamburg-Fuhl Sbuettel — Attached to Flieger- Ersatz-Abteilung 1.

Konder Werke — Grossenhain — Attached to Flieger-Ersatz-Abteilung 6.

Nordhausen a/Harz Attached to Flieger-Ersatz Abteilung?

Krefeld — Attached to Flieger-Ersatz-Abteilung?

L. V. Q. — Koselin — Attached to Flieger-Ersatz- Abteilung 8

N. F. W. — Gross-Zscnocher b/Leipzig — Attached to Flieger- Ersatz-Abteilung?

Rumpler — Muencheberg — Attached to Flieger-Ersatz Abteilung?

FLIEGER BEODACHTER SCHULEN (Observers School)

Fuerth i/Bayern
Gotha
Grossenhain
Hannover
Koenigsberg i/PR
Lager Lechfeld

Schwerin
Schleissheim
Stolp
Thorn
Warschau (dissolved

ARTILLERIE FLIEGER SCHULEN
(Artillery Observers School)

Jueterbog
Libau (dissolved)
Grafenwoehr (a small Bavarian Artillery Observers school)

FLIEGER FUNKER SCHULEN (Wireless Telegraphy School)

Neu Ruppin
Schleisheim
Stolp (dissolved)
Warschau (dissolved)
Johannisthal

FLIEGER FUNKER VERSUCHSANSTALT
(Wireless Telegraphy Experimental Station)

Doeberitz

BOMBEN LEHR ABTEILUNG (Bombing School)

Frankfurt a/o

BOMBEN VERZUCHE ABTEILUNG
(Bombing Experimental School)

Frankfurt a/o
Doeberitz

SPEZIAL KAMPF-EINSITZER SCHULEN
(Single-seater schools at home)

These schools have been dissolved as pilots who have passed the third examination were trained on single-seater at the Flieger-Ersatz-Abteilungen. The Fokker school at Schwerin has been dissolved.

GESCHWADER SCHULEN,

Paderborn
In 1917 a Geschwaderschule existed at Freiburg i/Br.

JAGDSTAFFEL SCHULEN

Two in the Army zone, their position was constantly changed.

FLIEGER SCHUTZEN ZUGE
(Machine Gunners Section)

Attached various Flieger-Ersatz-Abteilungen and Observers Schools Flieger Schutsen Zuges were known to exist at the following places:-

Boblingen Freiberg (in 1917) Hannover Schwerin Gotha
Lager Lechfield Schleissheim

PRUFANSTALT UND WERFT (P. U. W.)
(Experimental and testing stations)

Aldershof By far the most important.
Doberitz

FLUGZEUGMEISTEREIEN
(Aircraft Depots and Testing Stations)

Aldershof
Charlottenburg
Bork
F. T. Rustkommando (F. T. Rust) (Wireless Telegraphy Station)
Berlin I
Moteren Schulen (Motor Schools)
Benz & Cie Mannheim
Mercedes Stuttgart

Maybach	Friedrichshafen
Oberusel	Reinickendorf b/Berlin
Argus	Cannstatt Magnet Schule
Bosch	

MARINE LANDFLIEGER UND MARINE BEOBACHTER SCHULE

Johannisthal

Owing to the very large amount of flying carried out at Johannisthal Army flyers are no longer trained there.

RIESENFLUGZEUG ERSATZ ABTEILUNGEN.

Koln a/Rh

Doberitz

HEIMAT SCHUTZ-STAFFELN.

(Rheinland and Ruhr district)

The following were known to exist in 1917.

Freiberg i/Br	Boblinghen	Karlsruhe	Mainz	Gonzenheim
Koln a/RHein	Essen	Dortmund	Dusseldorf	

NORDSEE KUSTENSCHUTZ

(North Sea defence squadrons)

Gesstemunde Elbemundung (mouth of the Elbe) Tondern

NACHRICTEN ERSATZ ABTEILUNGEN

Or the First of April 1918 eightenn Neas were formed out of the Telegrafen Butaillonen and the Flieger Funker Kommandos. Nachricten Ersatz Abteilungen were known to exist at the following places:-

Nachricten Ersatz Abteilung - 1 Treptow-Berlin
Nachricten Ersatz Abteilung - 6 Breslau
Nachricten Ersatz Abteilung -10 Hannover
Nachricten Ersatz Abteilung -10 Verdun a/Alder
Nachricten Ersatz Abteilung -17 Hammerstein i/Westpreussen
Nachricten Ersatz Abteilung -? Saarlouis
Nachricten Ersatz Abteilung -? Kottbus
Nachricten Ersatz Abteilung -14 Karlsruhe

All telegraphists, telephonists, signallers, wireless telegraphy operators and aeroplane wireless telegraphy operators are trained at the Nachrichten Ersatz Abteilungen. (The latter until they are drafted into a Flieger Funker Schule).

The instructors were nearly always engineers with a University degree. After a course of lectures on elementary physics and the principles of electricity, special instruction was given on telegraphy and wireless telegraphy. There was special training for wireless telegraphy operators in the trenches, for wireless telegraphy operators in battle stations, on aeroplanes, in central stations and wireless telegraphy mechanics. The average pupil reached the required speed of 80 letters per minute sending and receiving after three months, training. Many pupils however reached a speed of 100 to 120 letters per minute. Although receiving and transmitting form the greatest part of the training, practice in the erection of Wireless Telegraphy apparatus and night practices in similar conditions to those obtaining on the front with a make-shift installation of the station are constantly hold. All messages sent during any practices were invariably sent in code.

TRAINING OF WERKMEISTER

The Werkmeister is the equivalent of the Equipment Officer in the Royal Air Force but he is not a commissioned officer, he was usually an offizier-stellvertreter. In 1916 an order came out that only mechanics that had passed through the course at the Werkmeisterschule were to be appointed Werkmeister. Since that date the training of Werkmeister was arranged as follows:-

First mechanics (always N.C.Os) that had proved exceptionally efficient were sent home to their Flieger-Ersatz-Abteilung as Werkmeister Aspiranten. Thereafter being employed in the Werftkompagnie for a short time, they had to pass a preliminary examination and were then sent to the Werkmeisterschule at Adlershof for an eight weeks course. Werkmeister were not invariably men from units at the front although this was the rule. The examinations at the end of the course were fairly difficult, far greater knowledge and ability was now required in 1918 than in 1914. In 1916 and 1917 a large number of mechanics passed the Werkmeister examination more than could be employed and many of them were still employed as assistant Werkmeister as there were not sufficient vacancies on the establishment.

FLAK SCHEINWERFER ZUGE (AA Searchlight Sections)

In April 1918 there was an A. A. Searchlight section of 8000 men in Hannover. This section was only used for training purposes.

E.C. Kny, designer, with DFW Monoplane 1913. These designs did not last the rigours of war and were soon replaced

AEROPLANES

By late 1916 the serial number carried by a German Army aircraft indicated the manufacturer, the type of machine (purpose), the airframe registration number (Bestellnummer), the year in which it was ordered and the name of the manufacturer if the machine had been licence built. It was not uncommon for the serial number to be completely or partially obliterated by the pilot's personal motif or a unit marking. In August 1914 the German Army had many first line aircraft, most of which were biplanes. Of the monoplanes the initial majority were of the 'Taube' types. Many Taubes (Doves) were built by other manufacturers and the term described a design type based on an original design by the Austrian Etrich. The Taubes varied in detail but all conformed to the same basic pattern of a shoulder wing, externally braced monoplane, with the distinguishing feature of a bird shaped wing and tail shape. The early two seaters had the observer at the front and the pilot at the rear. (Reminiscent of a chauffeur in a coach with horses.)

Jeannin Taube 1914

The Taube's, although very graceful in flight, were slow and quite unsuitable for military purposes, nevertheless these machines and the Albatros biplanes were the most common types of German aircraft seen during the opening months of the Great War. The first serial number allocated to these early types indicated the class of machine, the order number and the year in which the machine had been ordered. The monoplanes were classed as type 'A' machines and the biplanes as type 'B': examples include a Jeannin Taube numbered A 271/ 14 and an Albatros B.1 numbered B 848/ 14. From early 1915 the Taubes began to fade away from the battlefield and the remaining machines were mostly two-seat biplanes of the 'B' type although a few monoplanes of Fokker and Pfalz construction were used for one purpose or another.

In mid-1915 a new type of two-seater biplane appeared at the front armed with a machine-gun fitted to a gun ring for use by the observer who now set behind the pilot. The appearance of these machines reflected the changing pattern of the war on the Western Front and they were given the new classification of 'C' types. They replaced the earlier 'B' types which were relegated to training duties. Later C types also carried a fixed forward-firing machine-gun for the pilot's use. The advent of the Fokker monoplane fitted with a machine-gun in late 1915 led to the Introduction of a new classification, the single-seat armed fighting monoplane. Until it was fitted with a gun, the Fokker was classified as the A.lll. It now became the E. I and other armed single seat machines were also placed in this class (e.g. the Pfalz). Eventually, in early 1916 the Fokker monoplanes were outclassed by the superior Allied types appearing at the front (such as the DH 2) and the need for a single-seat armed biplane scout (the term 'fighter' was not used at this time and "Scout" remained in use until the end of the war). The requirement for a biplane scout as opposed to a monoplane, despite the success of the Fokker Monoplane series was not unusual, for a biplane offered the superior qualities of manoeuvrability and climb as opposed to the poorer performance of the monoplane of that period.

The new type designation "D" was introduced and this classification remained in use for biplane scouts until 1918 when it was applied to the Fokker D.VIII parasol monoplane which had originally been classified as the E.V. In early 1917 a new type of fast two-seater had been envisaged for escort duties in units to be known as Schutzstaffeln. These machines were to be lighter in construction than the usual two-seater of the C type and were to have a performance corresponding to their duties. These machines, given the class designation 'CL', were, however reorganised into Battle Flights (Schlachtstaffelnl) and were used in offensive roles. The most outstanding machines in this class were the Halberstadt CL II and the Hannover CL 11/ 111. Later in the war armoured machines, specifically designed for trench strafing and close support work were introduced and were given the classification 'J'. AEG and Gotha-Ursinus types had been used in limited numbers since early 1915 and because of their size they were called Grossflugzeuge and classified as 'G' types. The very earliest attempts by the Germans to build very large four-engined machines resulted in these being also classed as Gs but they were later reclassified as 'R' types. The best known examples of these being the enormous Zeppelin Staaken 'Giants', the 'R' signified 'Riesenflugzeuge' (literally Giant aeroplane). The classification G was then reserved solely for twin-engined bombers of Gotha, AEG, Friedrichshafen and Rumpler types. In service however, other terms were used such as the manufacturer's production. 'DO' abbreviation for 'Doppeldecker' and merely means 'two wings', or biplane. It was a pre-war term but was often used in the early days of the war. 'M' Indicates 'Militarmaschine' or military aircraft. Sometimes used by a manufacturer (e.g. Fokker) to indicate that the machine was designed specifically for military purposes although frequently the aircraft was no different from the original. 'E' Indicates 'Eindecker' or single-wing machine (monoplane) which is self-explanatory. Some firms used this with a prefix indicating the manufacturer (e.g. Gotha LE 3 Taube). The letter could also indicate 'Einsitzer' or single-seater. 'K' Usually an abbreviation for 'Kampf' or "Kampfer:" meaning fighting machine. The first twin engined AEG was designated K.1. It might also mean 'Krieg' (War) in some cases.

Entente Intelligence sources at this time referred to the various types of German machines according to the year in which or was supposed to have been designed. In consequence machines were referred to as the 1914 type Albatros or the 1915 model Fokker etc. Apart from this, aircraft were sometimes referred to by their manufacturer's model number and this can lead to confusion. For example, the Junkers armoured biplane which arrived at the front in 1917 was given the Army classification of 'J' and it became known as the J. 1. Unfortunately the letter 'J' was also the company's abbreviation and the same machine was the Junkers Company's product J.4. Similarly the same firm's J.10 low-wing two-seat monoplane attack machine of 1918 was given the Army classification of CL 1.

Many machines never developed further than a few prototype models and in consequence never received an Army classification. On the other hand, several did receive a military serial although they never went into production. Good examples of these are those single-seat scout prototypes which were submitted for the "D" type competitions towards the end of the war. Examples of these include the Daimler L6 which participated in the Aldershof competition of May-June 1918 under the designation of Daimler D.1 only about six of these machines were built.

Roland D.VI

Aircraft Type Codes

Prefix
Code Type of aircraft

A. (1911-1915) Unarmed two-seat monoplane principally Taubes, 568 built.

B. (1911-1918) Unarmed two-seat biplanes, by late 1915 usually indicated a training machine, 6191 built.

C. (1915-1918) Armed two-seat biplane; initially with one gun, later two and used for general observation, artillery spotting and occasional bombing purposes.

CL. (1917-1918) Two-seat biplane of lighter construction than C type armed and of superior performance (Later, monoplanes given this classification).

CLB. (1918) Late sub-classification for light armoured attack biplane 25057 built C, CL and CLB.

D. (1916-1918) Armed single-seat biplane, one or two guns. In 1918 was applied to monoplanes on the same class, 12207 built.

DJ. (1918) Late sub-classification; as for D but armoured for trench strafing.

Dr. (1917) Triplane aircraft, the fourth Fokker Triplane built was so designated (see F) 339 built.

E. (1915-1916, 1918) Armed single-seat monoplanes, mainly Fokker and Pfalz types 1028 built.

Albatross C.1

Halberstadt C.5

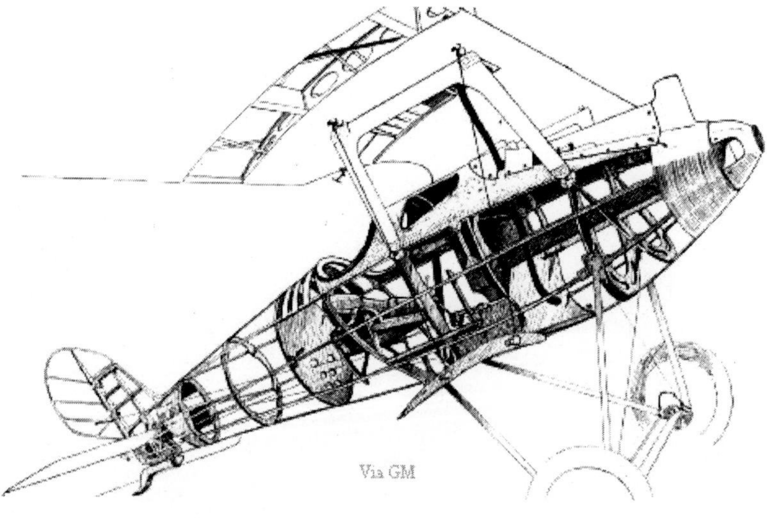

Pfalz D.III

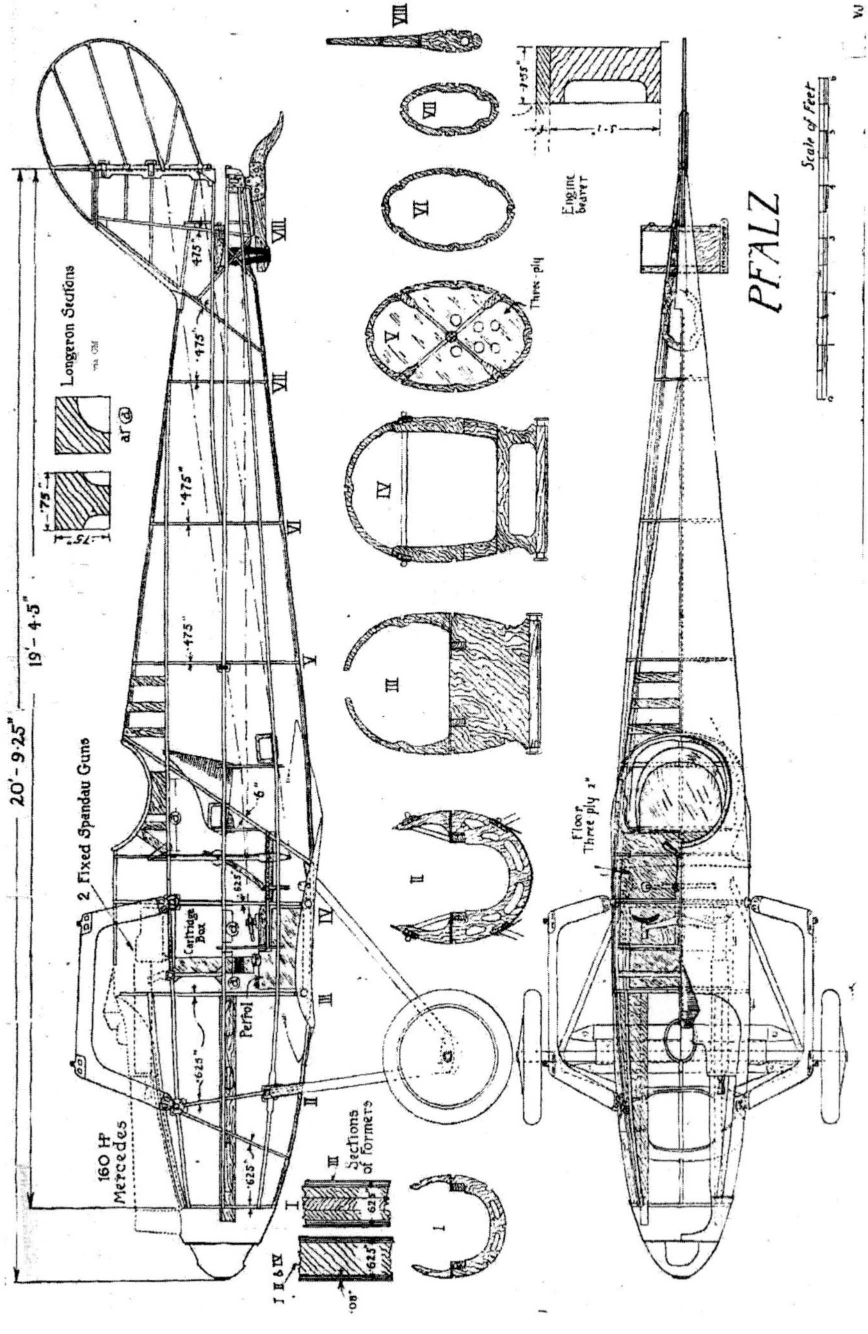
PFALZ
Scale of Feet
Engine bearer
Three-ply
Longeron Sections
2 Fixed Spandau Guns
Cartridge Box
Petrol
160 HP Mercedes
Sections of Formers
Floor Three ply 2"
20'- 9·25"
19'- 4·5"

F. Only applied to the first three Fokker Triplanes built also allotted for Civil Aeroplanes but not used.
G. (1915-1918) Initially all multiengine aircraft then specifically for twin engined bombers.
GL. (1917-1918) Late sub-classification of the twin-engined bomber type with lightened airframe 2028 built of G and GL types.
I. (1917-1918) 913 built
J. (1917-1918) Armoured two-seater biplane specifically designed for supporting ground troops.
N. (1916-1918) Late classification for a single-seat night bomber 204 built.
R. (1915-1918) (Riesenflugzeuge) Large multiengine bombing aircraft.
S. (Schlachtflugzeug) Late classification for a single-seat armoured ground attack machine two built.

Principal Source: COMMISSION INTERALLIÉE DE CONTROLE AÉRONAUTIQUE EN ALLEMAGNE - Societe des Nations, translated CEM.

Aircraft Company Abbreviations

Military		Naval
AEG	Allegemeine Elektrizitats Gesellschaft, Hennlngdorf.	AEG
Ago	*Ago* Flugzeugwerke GmbH, Johannisthal. Berlin.	Ago
Alb.	*Albatros* Werke GmbH, Johannisthal, Berlin. Albatros Gesellschaft fur Flugzeugunternehmungen mbH Friedrichshafen (seaplanes).	Alb.
Av.	Automobil und Aviatik AG, Leipzig-Heiterblick.	
Bay	Bayerische Flugzeugwerke A. G. Munich	
Bayru	Bayerische Rumplerwerke G.m.b.H. Augsburg	
Br.	Hansa und *Brandenburgische* Flugzeugwerke, AG, Brandenburg am Havel.	Br.
Daim.	*Daimler* Motoren Gesellschaft Werke Sindelfingen	
Dfw	Deutsche Flugzeug-Werke GmbH. Lindenthal bei Leipzig.	
Eul.	*Eulerwerke.* Frankfurt am Main.	
Fok.	*Fokker* Flugzeug-Werke GmbH, Schwerin-Gorries, Mecklenburg.	
Fdh.	Flugzeugbau *Friedrichshafen* GmbH, Manzell and Warnemunde (repair work at Warnemunde only) Zeppelin subsidiary.	FF
Germ.	Germania Flugzeugwerke G. m. b. H. Leipzig-Mockau	

Manufacturing aircraft wings

Removing a Pfalz fuselage from a mould

Installing aero-engines in fighters at the Pfalz aircraft factory

Working on a Pfalz tail and wings

Manufacturing an Albatross fuselage and wings

Doping Fokker wings and completing a Fokker D.VII

Moving a Pfalz fuselage into the factory for completion

Testing an aero-engine

Fitting an engine cowl on a Pfalz Scout

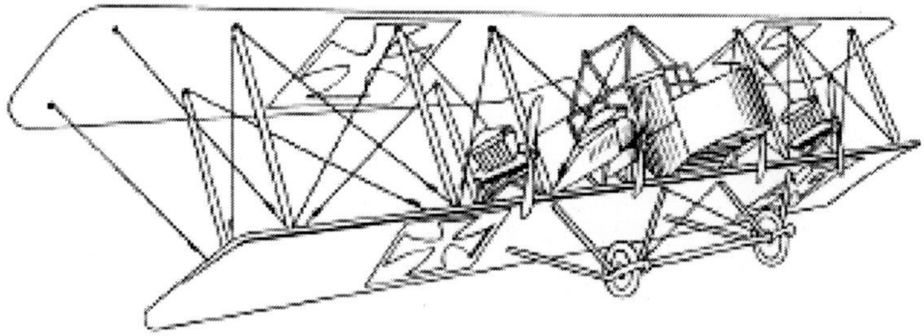

Siemens Schuckert Bomber inspired by Sikorski

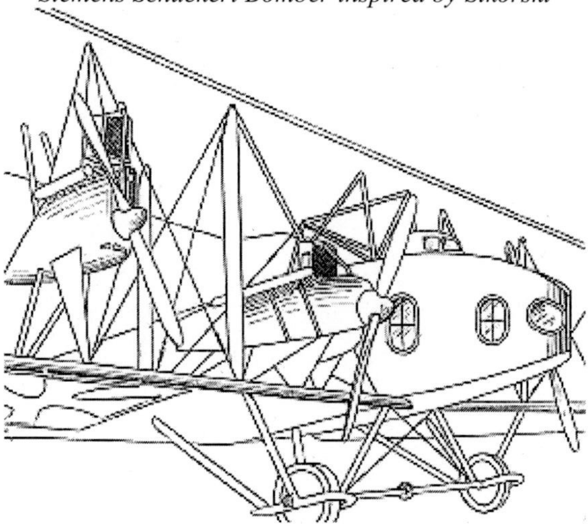

Later Siemens Schuckert Riesenflugzeuge bomber

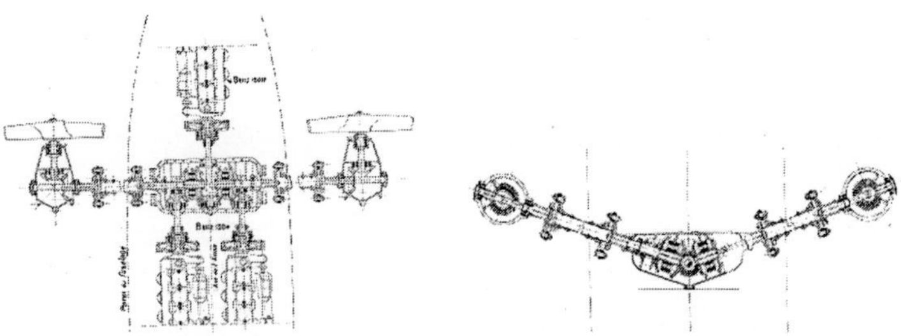

Siemens Schukert aircraft engines arrangement

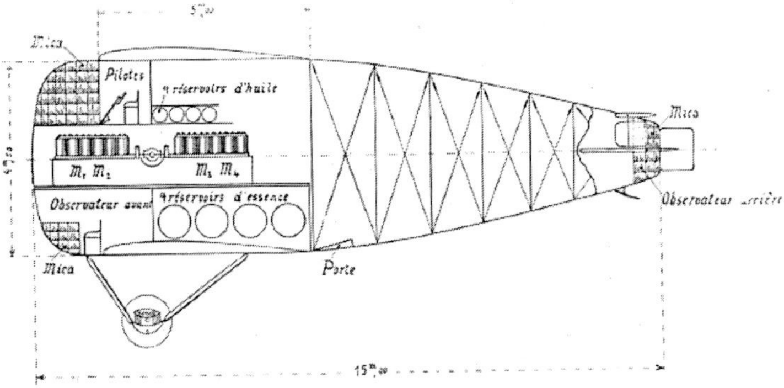

Link-Hoffmann Riesenflugzeuge Type R40/16

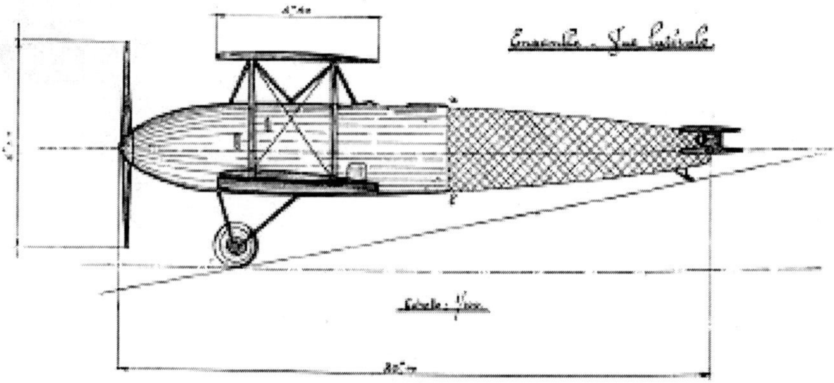

Link-Hoffmann Riesenflugzeuge Type R55

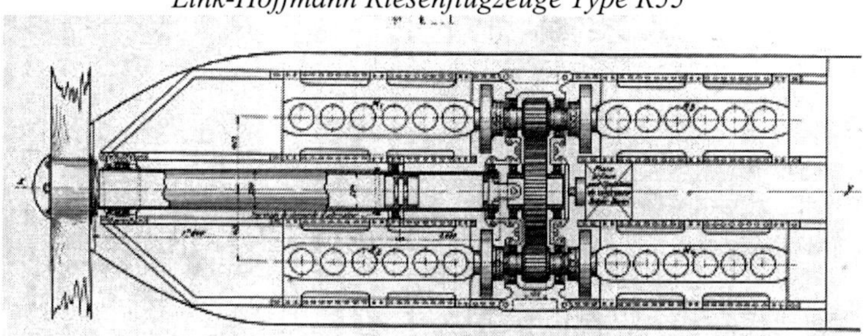

Link-Hoffmann Riesenflugzeuge Type R55machinery arrangement

Go. Gothaer Waggonfabrik AG *Gotha.* Go
Halb. Halberstadter Flugzeugwerke GmbH. *Halberstadt*

Hn. Hannoversche Waggonfabrik AG, Hannover-Linden –
(known as 'Hawa' for short).
Hansa Hanseatische Flugzeugwerke, A. G. Karl Caspar
Fühlsbüttel bei Hamburg
Junk *Junkers* Flugzeug-Werke AG. Dessau. Junk
Kaiserliche Marlnewerft GmbH, (Imperial Dockyards) KW
Danzig, Kiel and Wilhemshafen.
Kon Kondor Flugzeugwerke G. m. b. H. Essen-Ruhr

Li. Linke und Hoffman Werke AG Breslau.
Rol. Luftfahrzeug Gesellschaft m.b.H. (LFG), Berlin- LFG
Charlottenburg Bitterfeld and Stralsund (seaplanes).
(Aircraft called *Rolands)*
LVG Luft-Verkehrs Gesellschaft mbH. Johannisthal bei Berlin
Oertz-Werke GmbH, Reiherststieg bel Hamburg. Oertz
Mark Mârkische Flugzeugwerft Golm in der Mark
Mer Merkur Flugzeugbau G. m. b. H. Berlin
Oaw Ostdeutsche Albatros-Werke GmbH, Schneidermuhl.
Pfal. *Pfalz* Flugzeug-Werke GmbH, Speyer a/Rhein.
Rat. Waggonfabrik Jos. Rathgeber München-Moosach
Rin. Albert Rinne Flugzeugwerke Berlin-Rümmelsburg
Ru. *Rumpler* Flugzeug-Werke GmbH, Johannisthal Berlin. Au.
Sab. *Sablatnig* Flugzeugbau GmbH. Berlin. Sab.
Schul. Luftfahrzeugbau *Schutte-Lanz,* Mannheim-Rheinau
also at Zeesen bel Konigswursterhausen. Ssw.
Ssw *Siemens-Schuckert* Werk GmbH, Berlin and Nurnburg.
Flugzeugwerke *Lubeck-Travemunde* GmbH Trav.
Fok. Schweriner-Industrie werke G. m. b. H Schwerin-Goeries
Zeppelin-Werke GmbH, Lindau. Lindau and Seemoos Do. Do.
(Dornier, Giant 'R' flying boats).
Staak. Zeppelin-Werke *Staaken* GmbH. Staaken bel Berlin
(Giant 'A' landplanes). Staak
Torp. Luft-Torpedo Gesellschaft Berlin

Ot. Ottowerke G. m. b. H. Munich Goedecker Flugzeugwerke Mainz.

Main German companies which repaired aircraft or built aircraft accessories during the Great War.

1. Franz Schneider Flugmaschinenfabrik, G. m. b. H. Seegefeld bei Spandau.
2. Richard Goetze Flugzeugwerke G.m.b.H. Treptow Elsenstr. 106/107 et Flugplatz Johanisthal.
3. Nordeutsche Flugzeugwerke G.m.b.H. Teltow-Berlin
4. Otto Werke-München G. m. b. H. Schleissheimerstr. 141
5. Otto Schwade und C° Erfurt
6. Arsenaux, Reichswerft Kiel, Reichswerft Wilhelmshafen, R eichswerft Dantzig
7. G. Kuhles Thuringen
8. Grotian Steinweg Braunschweig 24/Zimmerst.
9. Burkart und Gunther Hameln a/Weser.
10. Mechanische Werksttâten für Flugzeugindustrie Berlin Lichtenberg 268 Frankfurterallée.
11. Astro Flugzeug-industrie Steglitz. Weissenweg 10
12. Triton Werke A. G. Schanzenstr 75/77 Hamburg
13. Volthain Seil und Kabelwerke Francfort
14. Berliner Metall Industrie Néanderstr 4 Berlin
15. Flugzeug Industrie Jôstadt-Sachsen
16. Hagona und Lehmann Leipzig
17. Eisengièsserei Hugo Stoss Ettishoferstr 5/Weingarten.Würtemberg
18. Karl Merkelbach Robertmayerstr. 52/Francfort
19. Heinrich Glaser Dresde
20. Norddeutsche Kühler Fabrik Friedrichstr 225/Berlin
21. Neue Industrie Werke Oberürsel
22. Haake Flugzeugwerke Johannisthal Friedrichstr. 3
23. Deutsche Luft Reederei 1° Johannisthal D. L. R. 2° Leipzig-Germania Werke 3°Warnemünde an der Ostsee

Fokker E.III Eindecker

L.V.G. C.II

Aviatik C.II

Albatross B.II

Halberstadt D.II

Albatros C III (DFW) 1918

A.E.G. G.II

Pfalz D.III

Gotha G.V

Fokker D. VIII (E.V.)

Fokker D. V.II (OAW) 2052-18
(Possibly in Entente hands)

Fokker Triplane

The supreme aero-product of the German aircraft industry, the Zeppelin Staaken, the first modern all-metal airliner

Staaken interior

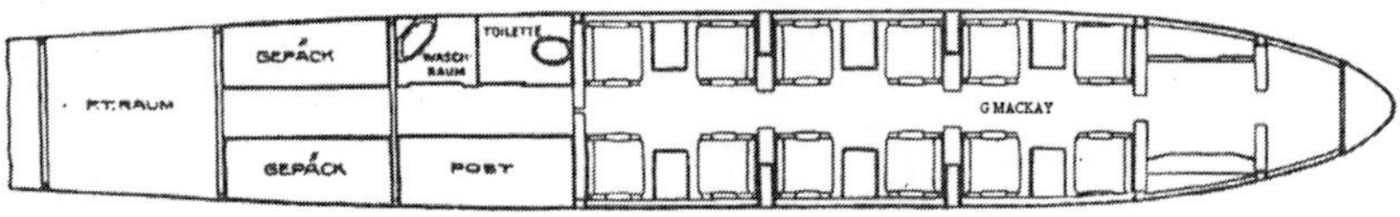

Staaken plan view of fuselage

Designed by Adolf Rohrbach in March 1919 and first flew in September 1920, using engines supplied by the Entente. Used all the experience of German giant aircraft in wartime When grounded fitted with a cockpit canopy, engineless airframe destroyed January 1921.

National Insignia and Camouflage

The Iron Cross, the Cross Patee, was used as the national markings on German aircraft from August 1914 of the war until around 20 March 1918, when it was replaced by the Greek cross or "Balkankreuze." This was for Operation Michael, the spring offensive on the Western Front. The Germans had the same national markings in all the normal airframe positions with the cross at the tail occupying both fin and rudder. On early aeroplanes, completed in a natural finish, a black cross on its own was sufficiently conspicuous. With the introduction of printed fabrics and camouflage, white edging or a white square field was used to give contrast to the black cross. The proportions of the cross itself and the edging, varied on many aircraft but as a general rule national insignia were consistent throughout any one machine.

An Albatross fighter was shot down on the morning of 14 April 1918 which bore the new type of Greek cross. The new cross had been made by painting out the flaring corners of the Maltese cross with which the aircraft had been formerly marked. Then eleven days later German aircraft were seen over the Belgian front marked with rectangular black crosses in a white circle instead of the usual Maltese cross. When the order was first put into operation it was found that the new insignia led to confusion and three German aviators were said to have been victims of the change. As a consequence the Chief of Aviation of the VII Army ordered the flights under his command to discontinue the change. Numerous reports were sent to the Aviation Section at General Headquarters, and on April 17, when prisoners were interviewed, there was a feeling of certainty that the order would be revoked and that the Maltese cross would be used again.

During July 1918, a Rumpler was intercepted by a Spad over Bernecourt while it was photographing the front lines. The fuselage and engine were painted a light red, upper surfaces of the wing were bluish with black crosses outlined in yellow at each wing tip. The Rumpler had a yellow tail with a black cross. Then on 13 September 1918 a formation of Spad fighters were attacked by a total of seven Fokker D.7s. The pilot's reported that the Fokkers were painted dark brown with black crosses but the tails were painted black with whited crosses.

Early German aircraft had a pale cream factory finish which in service often deteriorated to a greyish-white colour. This applied to early pre-1916 Aviatik, Albatros and D.F.W. biplanes and Fokker monoplanes. In

German Aircraft Insignia
August 1914 to March 1918

Bottom markings from around 19 March 1918 to the Armistice
Used on all standard positions

1916 some airframe fabrics in their natural off-white colour were printed with a close pattern of black dots giving an overall grey shade at a distance. Also in 1916 a true camouflage scheme was introduced by spray-painting blotches of green purple and brown over upper-surfaces, this was applied to observation aircraft types. A merging line of upper-surface brown, green and purple into a grey or blue-grey under-surface occurred about a foot below the fuselage datum line on the Pfalz and Albatros round sectioned fuselages.

Printed fabrics were introduced in 1917 with a four- to six-colour scheme in a mosaic pattern of lozenges, hexagons or irregular shapes. Colours were yellow, green, pink, brown, blue and black for 'D' class aircraft with an 'elongated hexagon' style pattern. 'G' class aircraft fabric were patterned with regular hexagons, in sage green, reddish mauve, bluish mauve, black, blue and grey. Some bombing squadrons considered the fabric colours too harsh and retouched the brighter colours in grey.

Large bombing aircraft often had a dual scheme, for the printed fabrics were of poor quality and not considered suitable for the lifting surfaces.

There was a trend with certain aircraft types which can be seen on A.E.G. machines, particularly the CIV type, which were given a sprayed camouflage and the firm's trade mark was marked on the rudder. Albatros CIII biplanes had a square white field for national markings; later DV and DVa scouts had a dark varnish on the plywood covered fuselage with wings and tail unit in a mosaic pattern fabric. Fokker EI, II, III and IV monoplanes had a clear finish and Fokker DVII and DVIII scouts, usually a mosaic patterned fabric throughout; one known exception, a clear white Fokker DVII fighter, marked with 'Fok. DVII F5125/18' along the bottom edge of the fuselage side; this aircraft was flown by a pilot destined to become head of the Second World War Luftwaffe-Reichmarshal Goring.

Hannoveraner biplanes had the mosaic patterned fabric for all surfaces including fabric over the plywood skin of the fuselage. Pfalz DIII scouts with ply-covered fuselages were often painted silver over-all except for the aluminium engine cowling which was given various colours. Generally L.F.G. Roland machines had a finish of purple, brown and green camouflaged upper-surfaces, with an under-surface light grey. Though some had a "duck egg blue" finish overall e.g. Roland C11.

Components such as cowlings, struts and fittings were painted at the manufacturer's discretion, grey being usual colour. Instructions were however issued to firms concerning colour coding control and piping systems. Petrol pipes were always white with small arrows at two foot intervals indicating the direction of flow. Other pipes were in blue and control cables and runners in grey.

Armament

Germany decided early that machine guns would play a dominant role in war and concluded from secret tests, that the Maxim machine gun, as it was still known in Germany, was the most reliable firing mechanism yet designed. The Model '08 Maxim was adopted as its first line machine gun. A later refinement of the standard '08 model resulted in a lighter version known as the '08/15. This water-cooled weapon was still fairly heavy and its 50-round belt with container could be attached on the side. A shoulder stock was also added together with a lightweight bipod of 2½ pounds. The total weight without water but with bipod was 31 pounds. The '08/15 differed from the '08 gun principally by its method of cooling. On this version the water jacket was simply filled and the jacket plug screwed in. There was no way to circulate the water as provided for in the heavier gun. This machine gun was produced in unusually large quantities as its modification from the original '08 model was comparatively easy. Entente intelligence agents estimated that at the outbreak of the war Germany had at least 12500 Maxim-type guns stored in huge warehouses and 50,000 more on order.

The '08 and '08/15 models were both used extensively in arming Zeppelins against hostile aircraft. But with all their planning and intrigue, the Germans did not foresee the incendiary bullet and its effects. The British shot the Zeppelin out of the sky by puncturing its huge hydrogen-filled envelopes with incendiary bullets. Germany similarly developed the Maxim machine gun for aircraft use, along with its successor, the lightened LMG 08/15 and apart from early experiments these guns were the only types of fixed forward-firing aircraft guns used by the German Air Force.

German Maxim machine guns were made in several factories but these aircraft versions were all made at a government weapons factory in Spandau, a suburb of Berlin; the discovery of the name 'Spandau' on the machine gun's nameplate led the Entente to call it by this name, although it was not an official designation. At the end of the Great War the Maxim gun was further modified to the MG 08/18, a lightened air-cooled weapon with a slim jacket.

The Spandau Gun, known as the Maxim LMG 08/15 was deployed by the German Air Service as a replacement for the Parabellum Gun which could not be used in the forward position on an aircraft. (The name

Spandau fitted to Fokker Eindecker

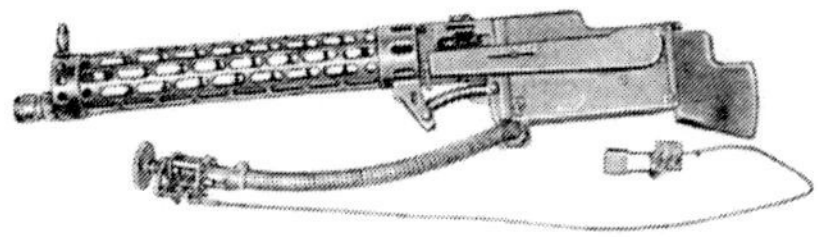

Spandau aircraft gun

Fitting a Spandau to a Pfalz

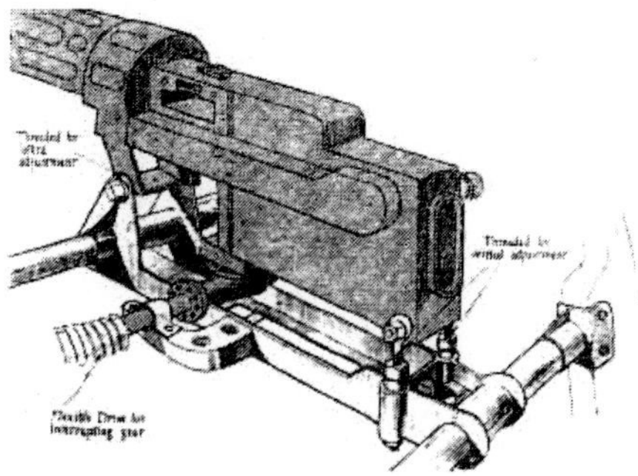

Spandau fitted to a Pfalz D.III

Parabellum

Parabellum being fitted to a gunner's cupola

'Parabellum' is Latin for 'prepare for war' was derived from the classical tag meaning 'if you wish for peace, prepare for war'.) The Parabellum had proved not to be suitable for use with the Fokker Interrupter Gear. Weighing 12kg - somewhat heavier than the Parabellum - the Spandau Gun had a theoretical cyclic firing rate of 500, 7.92mm rounds per minute. Production of the gun increased rapidly throughout 1916 with some 23000 produced by the Armistice. Key modifications over the Parabellum saw the removal of the stock, pistol grip and rear sight. The gun's water jacket was perforated to facilitate air cooling, later wartime models featured a purpose-designed air-cooling jacket. In order to allow the pilot to fly the aircraft with one hand while operating the gun with the other, the cocking and reloading device (the 'Klingstrom') was incorporated onto the right side of the weapon.

The German Government, a good many years before the war, had placed huge orders for machine guns with its main arms-producing factory, the Deutsche Waffen und Munitionsfabriken, located in Berlin. This company had unquestionably the greatest staff of gun experts to be found in the world. Its original head engineer had been an American, Hugo Borchard, the inventor of a pistol afterwards erroneously named for his assistant and successor, Georg Luger. Early in 1911 a gun designer, Karl Heinemann, joined the firm. He had already made a name for himself in the field of automatic weapons. Heinemann was given the all-important job of refining the Maxim machine gun. His resulting achievement was one of the most outstanding efforts to come from World War I. The German Army, committed to the Maxim gun which was already under production, specified the mechanism must be of this type. The Army requested a lightweight high-speed gun that would fire the same 7.9-mm Mauser cartridge as did its heavy machine guns and infantry rifle. To make a definite improvement on such a time and battle-tested weapon required the utmost skill and Karl Heinemann proved equal to the task. The product of his work was labelled the "Parabellum," which was the code name of the D. W. M. plant when referred to in correspondence. This superb weapon, like so many of its contemporaries in other countries, did not attract the attention it deserved until the necessity of war gave it a place among the finest automatic firing mechanisms of its time. Heinemann made the toggle joint break up instead of down, as in the original Maxim. The return spring was placed centrally against the crank and stored energy during the recoil stroke. The act of feeding was

Free gun mounting

Tourelle from Rumpler

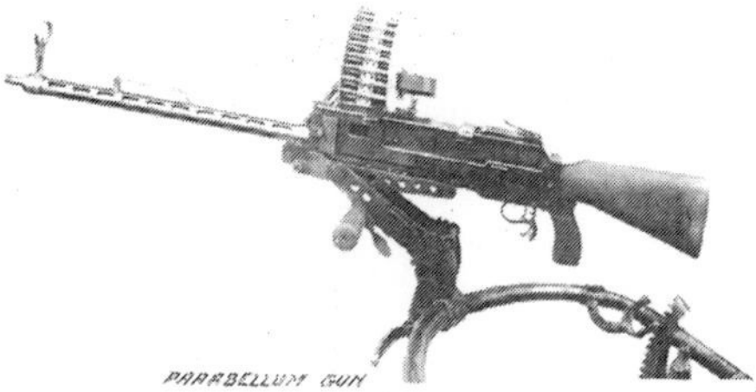

Parabellum

Tourelle for Halberstadt

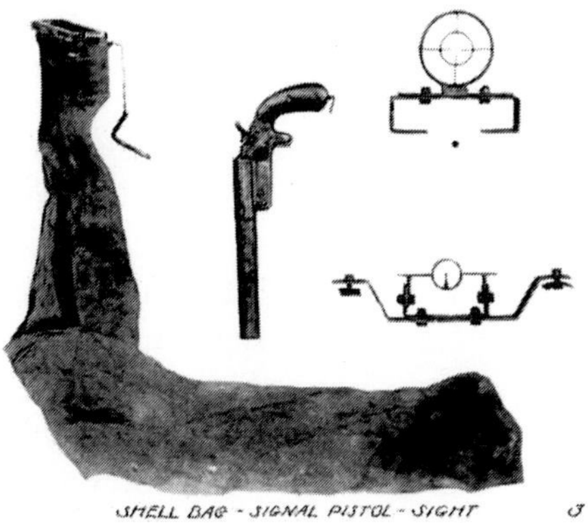

Flare pistol and ammunition bag with gun sights

Gotha Bomb Sight

performed by a pawl working off the lock instead of by vertical movement of the lock itself. A differential action was also incorporated to speed up feeding of the next to the indexed round. This was done by forcing the barrel forward by cams before the recoiling lock had reached its extreme travel rearward. A faster rate of fire was made possible by such utilization of the feed pawl. The feed belt was made of cloth or fabric wound on a spool fastened to the gun's receiver, thus allowing it to swing with the gun. In contrast with the earlier model the fusee spring was not adjustable. This refinement by Karl Heinemann was the lightest Maxim-action gun ever designed. It weighed only 22 pounds without accessories, with a 700-round-a-minute rate of fire. Needless to say, it was the very thing the German Air Force was looking for when its Zeppelin threat was exploded by British machine-gun fire. The Parabellum was the German first-line aircraft machine gun throughout the war. A few have also been found equipped with water jackets for ground use or perhaps more logically for Zeppelin mounting.

Anthony Fokker's idea came when he was shown the crude gun arrangement of a French fighter plane which had been brought down when flown by Roland Garros. This fighter, a Morane-Saulnier, was unique with the strip fed Hotchkiss machine gun firing through the air screw. Its airscrew was protected by the steel bullet-deflectors invented by Saulnier. Garros then had been shot down. After examining the enemy device the Fokker Company produced an interrupter gear. The result was the interrupter gear designed by the Fokker engineers Leinberger, Hebel and Lubbe during July 1915. While he was acclaimed for his feat, his invention was presumably based on a patent issued in 1913 to Franz Schneider, the L.V.G. designer, a Swiss aeronautical engineer, who had offered his invention to the German Army as early as 1912. After examination, it had been rejected as unnecessary, since there was no possibility that the aeroplane would ever become a fighting machine. (LVGs patent is DE310396 dated 6 July 1917) At that time the Zeppelin so dominated the German mind as the perfect aerial weapon that the value of Schneider's patent could not be foreseen. It was only in an hour of desperation that Germany was provided with Fokker's version of the Schneider synchronizer. Patent litigation ensued and Fokker lost but never paid a royalty to Schneider as was the outcome of the case. Within 48 hours after examining the makeshift French device, the Fokker Company produced a

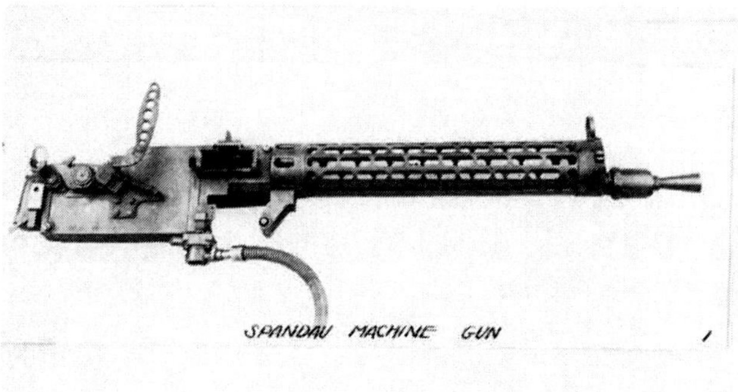

Spandau Machine Gun

SPANDAU GUNS AND SIGHT 2

Spandau Guns and Sight

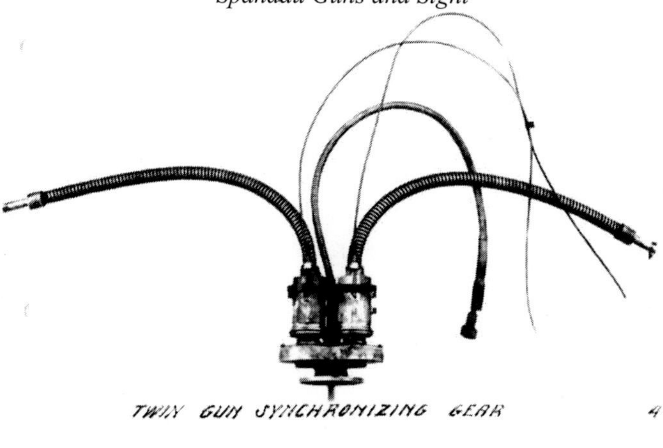

TWIN GUN SYNCHRONIZING GEAR 4

Twin Spandau interrupter gear Fokker pattern

reliable interrupter gear based on Schneider's patents. It added by a hundredfold to the deadliness of the superb fighting craft of his own design the Fokker M.5K (this became the Fokker E.1) when it was first fitted. The fitted machine gun was a Parabellum complete with wooden stock. The fact that Fokker had never handled a machine gun before in his life made this feat even more astonishing. The German staffs was highly incredulous that he could turn out anything worthwhile in so short time and Fokker gained its confidence only by repeated demonstrations with an aero engine fitted with his mechanism on the ground.

The first German pilot to use the synchronizer against the enemy was Lt. Oswald Boelcke, later to become Germany's pioneer ace because of this device. The next flyer to install one on his plane was Lt. Max Immelmann, also destined to become a great air fighter.

While there was great similarity between the German and the later British mechanical firing devices, except the Constantinescu type, the secret of the Fokker system was that the interrupter gear kept the trigger depressed while the propeller arc was clear. It let up on the sear at the approach of the leading edge of the blade which acted as an interrupter only in a burst. The British device worked just the opposite in that it tried to release the sear by a series of lugs striking cams. This allowed bullets to hit the blade if anything worked loose or if anything happened to change the timing of the weapon, since each individual impulse fired a shot. The German synchronizer fired a continuous burst except when the approach of the propeller and its corresponding lug on the shaft interrupted fire until the trailing edge of the blade had cleared.

The German fighter plane's propeller in normal flight rotated 1200 times per minute and as this made the blades pass a given place 2400 times, it can readily be understood that the timing device must be fool proof in design. With a 6-inch space passing a given point 2400 times a minute, the fundamental fact underlying the successful operation of any synchronizer is the relatively greater velocity with which the bullet is travelling to that of the turning blade.

The first Fokker planes, the EI, EII, and EIII, equipped with the interrupter gear, appeared on the Western Front in December 1915. They gave the Allies a decided setback and caused many casualties until something as efficient was produced as a countermeasure. The Spandau machine gun was only used as a synchronised gun for shooting to the front. The guns were equipped with two types of loading handle both of which produce a recoiling of the barrel simultaneous with the movement of the rolling handle. The loading handle is usually out of engagement with the roller handle by virtue of the gear segment being carried out of contact with the teeth on the roller handle hub in the position of rest. The roller handle can be worked independently for unloading and furthermore the normal functioning of the gun is not interfered with by the loading handle.

In most cases the gun used a Fokker interrupter gear operated by a flexible shaft. Usually the shaft was stationary but was only in motion during the actual firing of the gun. The trigger motor was so constructed that the guns do not fire until the clutch was fully engaged and ceased to fire when the clutch was disengaged. The clutches were thrown into gear by Bowden cables mounted on the pilot’s control column.

The gun was usually equipped with a shot counter mounted at the rear end of the gun and operated in the same manner as the British device used for the same purpose. About 25% of single seat German fighters had the guns equipped with counters. The rear of the Spandau guns were heavily padded and extended back into the pilot's cockpit. The metal ammunition boxes were crafted to each aeroplane with the provision of one or two for each plane. The rounds were carried in fabric belts but having no tabs extending beyond the belt. Each belt carried 550 rounds. The empty belt was carried through a metal chute to the lower part of the fuselage underneath the engine where it deposited used ammunition.

The Parabellum gun was used as a free gun on two-seater and bombing aeroplanes. A deep ammunition bag was used to gather loose rounds after the gun was fired; the bag reached the floor of the cockpit.

On both the Spandau and the Parabellum there was a small ring and bead site, the ring being at the muzzle of the gun. The diameter of the ring was too small to permit its use as a deflection sight. On two seat aircraft tourelles (cupolas) were installed made entirely of wood and were built into the fuselage. A number of variants existed, the simplest was a revolving ring having only a socket for the gun bracket and clamped in any position by a clamping handle which may be left in either the locked or unlocked position. The gun was carried on a vertical spindle which mounted a cradle at its upper end and additionally carried to the gun a reel for holding the belt of ammunition. Several cupolas had been built as copies of French and British types still having the wooden ring but using a metal tube in the form of an approximate semicircle which elevated and depressed the gun mounting. A counter balance was used, made of steel springs, to counter balance the weight of the gun. The elevating release and the ring releases were controlled by separate handles on the tube just to the left of the gun socket.

The Tourelles (Gunner's cupola) in German aeroplanes were not as efficient as those in Entente aeroplanes. It was found that it was awkward to have two different locks operated from different positions governing the elevating of the gun and the turning of the ring as the case may be.

Fighters were equipped with two Spandau guns and observation planes with one forward gun and one gun in the observer's tourelle. Many of the observation planes could be equipped with twin forward guns but invariably one was so fitted.

BOMBS

The first bombs that were dropped from the side of an aircraft were simply thrown overboard by hand and the target was chosen by the eye. There were no sighting devices yet, experience and practice perhaps also the size of the objectives had to be taken into account. It was probably around 1912 or 1913, as in France, that the problem of aerial bombardment and the development of sights were studied. The first German naval bombing tests took place in July 1913, on the occasion of Kiel Aviation Week; land planes were used and the target ship *Bayern* was used as the target. Later Specialised bombs were designed for use by aeroplanes and were all carried horizontally. Early in the war the only German aeroplane bomb being in use was a small pear-shaped bomb, which was carried in the fuselage and dropped by hand. Later, the idea of adapting shells for air dropping was adopted: vanes were fixed to a shell to ensure the bomb would strike the ground nose-first and to cause it to spin when it was dropped so that the fuse would function. The familiar bomb shape (pisceform) was evolved from this adaptation; the forward portion of the bomb and the nose fuse still retained their artillery shell markings.

Despite their many obvious shortcomings in a bomb fuse, the centrifugal bolts were persistently used as a safety device. The "gain", too, remained short (as in a shell fuse), until very late in the war, when an exploder running the whole length of the bomb was introduced in the 1000 kg bomb. It was immediately realised, however, that the heavy

casing of a shell was unnecessary and the 12 kg. (with, for a time, the 75 kg) was the only example of heavy case bomb in this series. In all cases the nose casing was made of heavy metal. The filling of these bombs, with slight variations, consisted of:-
Trinitrotoluene 60 %, Hexanitrodiphenylamine 40 %

With the largest German Aerial bomb the 1000 kg "Liebesgaben"

Bomb Types

12 kg. Bomb

Large numbers of these bombs were found on all air stations and bomb racks to carry them in all types of aeroplanes, proving them to be a most popular type of armament. Large bombers carried them, in addition to their heavy bombs and even fighters were fitted with a rack to carry four.

50 kg. Bomb

A new type of time fuse "Minenzeitzuhder" for this bomb appeared in 1918.

75 kg. Bomb

This was a heavy-case pisceform bomb, of approximately the same dimensions as the 50 kg bomb. Comparatively few of these bombs were found by the Entente forces and from that it would appear that whilst it was originally designed as a large bomb for use against personnel, it was later withdrawn in favour of the 12 kg bomb as the effective radius of the latter in comparison to the weight carried was considerably greater.

100 kg. Bomb

The fuses for this and the larger pisceform bombs were fitted with bifurcated strikers and twin detonators.

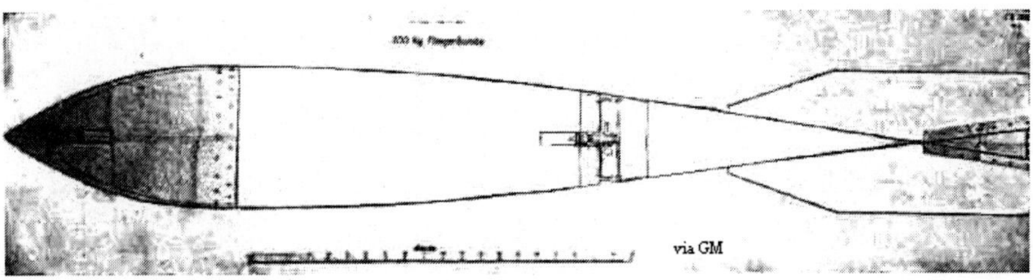

300 kg. Bomb

300 kg. Bomb

The fuses, though differing in size are similar in principle to those of the 100 kg bomb.

1000 kg. Bomb

The fuses though larger in size, were similar in principle to those of the 300 and 100 kg. bombs. Less than one hundred of these bombs were

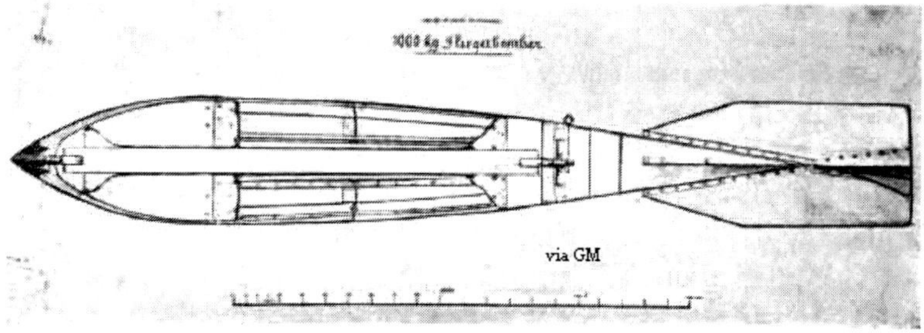

1000 kg. Bomb

found. Riesenflugzeuge (Giant Aeroplanes) were each intended carry two 1000 kg. and four 100 kg. bombs.

Incendiary Bombs

German incendiary bombs developed during the war along lines similar to those of the Entente countries: starting with a simple container for petrol with an ignition fuse and evolving through a combination of that with a chemical incendiary composition, to a small bomb of exceedingly fierce burning properties containing only an incendiary powder. As in the case of explosive bombs, incendiary bombs for aeroplanes, apart from the Elektron bomb, were pisceform in shape and were stowed horizontally, while those for airships were less elongated and were stowed vertically.

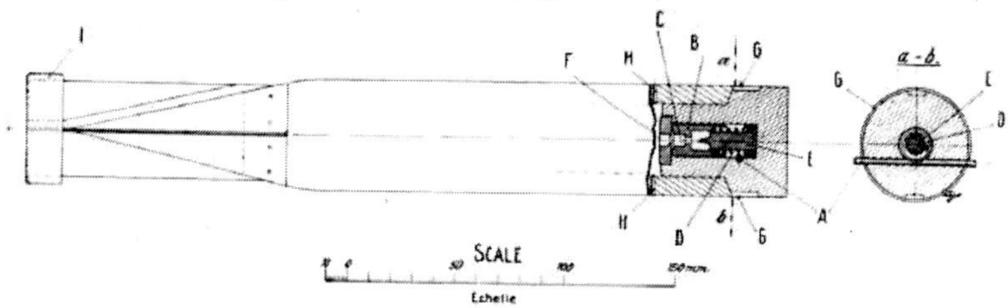

Elektron Incendiary Bomb

Elektron Incendiary Bomb

This bomb consisted of a cylindrical body of zinc and aluminium alloy, 1in thickness, 25 in long, and 5 in diameter. The top end was tapered off to take the tail portion carrying its vanes, which was affixed by means of six rivets. The lower end was threaded internally to take the fuse. The tail was formed of 3 sheet iron stampings, part of each being shaped to the cone of the tail, the other part forming a straight fin. The diameter of the tail and vanes was equal to that of the bomb; the tail was completed at the top by the addition of a narrow collar with a flange. The filling consisted of compressed thermite. A layer of igniting composition 1in thickness interposed between the thermite and the fuse. There were two vents (H) 3mm in diameter and 3.5mm from the bottom end of the bomb. Large numbers of these bombs, from which the Germans expected great results, were made during the second half of 1918 but none reached the front before the Armistice.

The Mouse Bomb

This was a small bomb, weighing 1 kg., specially designed for use against infantry and burst about 2’ 6” from the ground. It was first introduced in large numbers in June 1918 but was first reported by the British 22 May 1918. These little bombs were called the "Flying Mouse" and were only 4 or 5 inches long and slung on to carriers attached to the aircraft. As soon as one had been removed from its carrier, it was 'live' and had to be thrown overboard immediately. Their detonators were very sensitive and the bombs were therefore dangerous to handle. Four carriers, each bearing about six bombs, could be mounted on one aeroplane.

21cm Armour Piercing Bomb.

A number of these bombs were found in an Artillery Depot at Cuxhaven. They were apparently for use by seaplanes against battleships, the armour-piercing nose being designed to penetrate deck armour. No details were available for the Entente forces though the following details are known: Estimated weight 200 to 300 kg diameter 21cm Length 180 cm. These bombs were produced towards the end of the war and differed from any known type of German bomb. The shape was more perfectly streamline than usual. The material they were made from appeared to be cast steel. The bombs were divided in the exact centre; the tail portion contained the vanes screwing into the forward portion, which by itself has very much the appearance of a shell. The fuse was fixed in the base of the forward portion, from which a long tube extends, through the tail portion, to the end of the vanes. It was possible, that the forward portion of this bomb is an adaptation of a 21 cm shell, but if so, considerable alterations must have been made during the course of manufacture, if, indeed, the castings are similar. The bomb showed no sign of either driving band or canelure to contain same.

Anti-Submarine Bombs (U-Abwurf Bomben).

Several of these bombs were found at an Artillery Depot at Cuxhaven.

Specimens were sent to each of the Entente Powers. The following details are known:-

They were made in three sizes: 10, 30 and 60 kg. They were heavy case bombs made of cast iron. The vanes were attached from halfway down the bomb and rose in a continuous counter clockwise spiral to the top where they were protected by a circular band of metal. The vanes were not packed with the bombs but the latter had loose nuts to which the vanes were attached, apparently by the active service units using the bombs. The nose was threaded to take a fuse but no fuses were found. These bombs were old and very crudely made. It is thought, therefore, that they were an early type and soon to become obsolete, especially as only these few have been found and no traces of them, or gears to carry them, have been discovered on any of the German Seaplane Stations. Any of the light-case pisceform bombs with a delay action fuse would of course constitute a much more effective anti-submarine bomb.

Smoke Cloud, (Handnebelbombe).

The body of the bomb was a hollow sphere about 9 cm in diameter, nearly filled up with a cloud producing liquid. A tube containing a fuse and charge of black powder fitted into the sphere and projected outwards from it. The outer end of the tube was closed by a screw-on cover, which contained the knob and cord of a friction-tube igniter for the fuse. The flash from the cap ignited a slow burning charge, which communicated with another small igniter which acted immediately upon the black powder charge. The containing sphere appeared to be burst by the powder charge, the liquid contents being violently projected, so as to produce a large cloud. As its name and the friction-tube indicate, it was thrown by hand.

Parachute Flare

Parachute Flare

The parachute flare was a body of the shape and dimensions of an aeroplane incendiary bomb; its purpose was to illuminate the ground strongly from the air by night. The body was about 1 m. long and 10 cm in diameter, provided with 4 short flat vanes at the tail. The body and vanes were made of thin sheet iron. At the nose end was a clockwork time fuse protected by a clip-on bucket-shaped cover removed before dropping. The fuse cover was engraved with a height scale up to 7000 m. This was set before dropping, to a height 300 m. less than that indicated by altimeter. The flare then fell to within about 300 m. of the ground when the fuse acted and ignited a charge of black powder. The resulting explosion projected the contents of the flare-body out through the tail end. The contents consisted of a bundle of 5 cardboard tubes, fastened together, containing the illuminating charge. Each of the cardboard tubes terminated in a short length of fuse string and these strings were collected together in a wooden ring. There was also a thick wooden ring separating the powder charge of the fuse from the ends of the cardboard tubes. The centre of this ring contained a quantity of fuse string in short lengths. The black powder charge therefore besides projecting the illuminating charge out, set fire to the ends of the tubes. The bundle was supported in the air by a large parachute of black fabric, the supports being strings tied to rings sewn to the parachute. The strings were collected together by a cardboard disc, the final connection to the bundle of tubes being a chain attached to an eyelet in a metal disc screwed to the ends of the tubes. The flare body with the exploded fuse fell to the ground, leaving the flaming bundle of tubes suspended vertically from the parachute. The illuminating composition was a light grey powder, compressed into a solid mass. It appeared to consist largely of magnesium and burned for several minutes.

Types of German Bombs

TYPE OF BOMB	ACTUAL WEIGHT	EXPLOSIVE		TOTAL LENGTH	NUMBER AND LENGTH OF VANES	MAXIMUM DIAMETER	FUSES	CASING
		WEIGHT	PERCENTAGE TO TOTAL WEIGHT					
12 kg.	11 kg.	1,25 kg	11 %	75 c/m	3/34 c/m	9 c/m	Nose only	Heavy
50 »	55 »	20 kg.	37 %	170 c/m	3/50 c/m	18 c/m	—	Light
75 »	75 »	10 »	13 %	168 c/m	3/50 c/m	17 c/m	—	Heavy
100 »	91,5 kg.	53 »	58 %	187 c/m	4/54 c/m	25 c/m	Nose & Tail	Light
300 »	300 kg.	180 »	60 %	280 c/m	4/80 c/m	36 c/m	»	Light
1,000 »	1,080 »	643 »	60 %	390 c/m	4/122 c/m	35 c/m	»	Light

Roland Garros and the machine gun synchronising gear

In France, it had been recognized that the effectiveness of military aircraft would be increased if they were armed with machine-guns and that would mean a device enabled to be mounted on a tractor aircraft, firing forward through propeller. The first proposal to mount a machine-gun rigidly on an aircraft and align it by aiming the aircraft at a target was made by the German pioneer August Euler, whose patent (DE248601 of 23 July 1910) proposed the installation of a machine gun in a pusher aircraft. Then the Swiss engineer Franz Schneider, who had designed several of the early Nieuport monoplanes and had subsequently joined the German company L.V.G., wanted to make a fixed-gun installation in a tractor aircraft. His first thoughts were to install a gun to fire through a hollow airscrew shaft. He suggested to the Daimler Company that this could be done by inverting an in-line engine and fitting it with offset reduction gearing. Daimler built such an engine but it experienced much trouble from oiling of the spark plugs.

In 1913 Schneider secured, in the name of the LVG Company the German patent DE276396, 15 July 1913, in which he set out the basic idea of enabling a machine-gun to fire through a revolving airscrew by coupling its mechanism to the airscrew shaft. It is a remarkable fact that the Schneider patent was published, complete with explanatory diagrams, in the German journal FLUGSPORT on 30 September 1914, less than two months after the outbreak of war.

In arguments, designed to present Anthony Fokker as the true and only begetter of the synchronized machine-gun (which he was not), it has been stated that Schneider's device would not have worked. Had a gear been built exactly as described in the patent specification it probably would not have worked at the first attempt but Schneider had early in 1914 asked the German authorities for the use of a machine-gun m order to test his device, this request had been refused. Given proper testing facilities, an engineer of Schneider's calibre could hardly have failed to modify his mechanism appropriately. Had this happened Germany might have entered the war with her aircraft equipped with a synchronizing gear and there would have been nothing left for Fokker to "invent".

Possibly the earliest French patent relating to the firing of a machine-gun through a tractor airscrew FR475151 recorded on 22 January 1914 in the name of, "A.Deperdussin (representee par le syndic de faillite M. Raynaud) residant en France (Seine)." Basically this did little more than combine the advantages of a gun that could be arranged to fire through a revolving airscrew "by means of an electrical control or similar device": it did not describe any mechanism and obviously did no more than seek to protect the idea of arranging a gun in this way on a tractor aircraft.

The Deperdussin patent has some significance, however, because it envisaged the armouring of the airscrew blades as an alternative to the use of a synchronizing mechanism. As Deperdussin had been imprisoned on a charge of embezzlement, on 5 August 1913, he was in no position to undertake any development of his ideas. His patent had been applied for by the receiver appointed to administer the *Societe Provisoire des* AEROPLANES DEPERDUSSIN. Closely following the Deperdussin patent was an Italian patent applied for on 24 February 1914 by *Nieuport Macchi.* This was a little more thoroughly developed than the Deperdussin proposal but specifically envisaged a shaft taken from the rear of the engine driving, through bevel gears, a vertical shaft bearing and a cam that was expected to regulate the fire of the fixed gun. Far more significant than the Nieuport-Macchi device was the remarkably precise design for an *Avion de Guerre* patented by Robert Esnault-Pelterie. His patent application (FR475940) was made on 26 March 1914 and was intended to cover the design of a high- wing two-seat monoplane armed with two machine-guns, one firing forward through the airscrew disc, the other a movable gun covering the aircraft's tail. The crew were to be accommodated in an enclosed armoured cabin and Esnault-Pelterie even provided for a fixed safety frame to prevent the rear gunner from damaging his own aircraft.

This R.E.P. project intelligently anticipated several developments that were later compelled by the necessities of war and could be said to be the first design for a two-seat fighter aircraft. In this particular context its principal feature was the pilot's forward-firing gun. Although Esnault-Pelterie proposed that this gun should have some degree of movement. He included in his patent a well thought-out synchronizing mechanism that might well have been capable of being developed satisfactorily in an application to a fixed gun. He intended to install a rotary engine lying horizontally in the nose, bevel gears were to drive a horizontal shaft that carried the airscrew on its forward end and a further drive on its rearward extension; this in turn was to drive a shorter shaft that was linked to the firing mechanism of the gun.

It is doubtful whether Raymond Saulnier knew of the Deperdussin, Nieuport-Macchi or Esnault-Pelterie patents in April 1914 when he himself devised a synchronizing mechanism. The Deperdussin patent was not published until 23 April 1915, that of Esnault-Pelterie not until 24 June 1915; the French patent (FR477786A) covering the Nieuport-Macchi device was not applied for until 24 February 1915, a full year after the original Italian patent application was filed and was published in Paris on 8 November 1915. On 5 May 1914 Saulnier wrote to General Bernard, the Inspector General of Aeronautics, describing his proposal for the installation of a fixed machine-gun on a tractor aircraft; in particular, he outlined clearly the technique of aiming the aircraft armed in this way. Saulnier told the General that he would have a working installation ready for inspection in two to three weeks. His letter remained unanswered.

Writing in *l'Aerophile* of the 15 January 1926, Saulnier recorded this note:

"I invented the means of firing through the airscrew in April 1914 and Garros had no part in this invention. The drawings of the first synchronizing device were prepared in the design office of the Morane-Saulnier company, under the direction of Louis Peyret and the first actual firing trials were held on the range at the Hotchkiss works, near the Eiffel Tower, under the control of Colonel de Boigne a director of the Hotchkiss Company. Successful tests of the synchronization were made at an engine speed of about 1200 r.p.m. the grouping of the shots moved slightly as the engine speed varied. The device itself was satisfactory but was rejected because a few individual cartridges had abnormal explosion periods, consequently such rounds fired irregularly (incomplete/faulty load) and some of them, instead of falling into their appropriate group, struck the airscrew blade.

"To save time, I removed the linkage between the engine and the sear of the gun and tried a magazine of bullets at the airscrew, which I had protected with a metal deflector. Three types of deflector were tested in static trials.

"Meanwhile, the war had begun and the Hotchkiss machine-gun was withdrawn from me. Garros, who had immediately volunteered for military service left with his unit on 15 August for Verdun, subsequently moving to Dunkerque and sought me out in December 1914. Saying: 'I think your idea of firing through the airscrew is interesting and I have been allowed to come here to experiment and develop it.'

"It was then, with equipment provided by the Morane-Saulnier company (aeroplane, motor and bullet deflector) and with a machine-gun entrusted to him by the Minister of War, that Garros made the first true firing tests *in flight.* After this firing trial Garros got the Panhard company to make deflector for him. He had the ingenious idea of making them narrower by reducing the width of the airscrew blades at the points of attachment of the deflectors. Later in the war the deflectors were abandoned and the use of a synchronizing mechanism between the engine and the gun became universal."

Morane Saulnier propeller showing deflector plates. This is the example captured by the Germans.(JMB)

Roland Garros in the French Air Service

The principal reason for Saulnier's lack of success was as he describes, the unfortunate proportion of "hang-fire" rounds in the ammunition then available but the Hotchkiss gun was not ideally suited for synchronization because its firing pin was an integral part of the breech block.

On 5 February 1915 the *Societe des Aeroplanes Morane-Saulner* applied for French patent FR477530 for the design of an armoured airscrew for use on aeroplanes fitted with firearms. (Helice *blindee pour aeroplane pourvu d'arme a feu.)* This specifically embodied the reduced width of blade in line with the deflector *(l'helice prend une forme etranglee en une partie du pale, ce qui reduit la surface de la projection sur son plan),* the idea that Saulnier so rightly attributed to Garros.

In fact, the first device tested by Garros was appreciably more makeshift than Saulnier remembered (or perhaps ever knew). After Garros's death in action on 5th October 1918, there was found among his papers a note that he had prepared in reply to a letter written to him on 28 September 1918. This note is reproduced in full in Jacques Mortane's book *Roland Garros, genie du geste el de la pensee,* and must have been written by Garros on 4 October 1918. In it he relates how on his arrival at Villacoublay to undertake the task of developing the means of firing through the airscrew to a pitch of operational usefulness, he was given the third of four airscrews that Saulnier had fitted with armoured deflectors. According to Garros: “This primitive affair was not particularly successful: deflected bullets ripped the airscrew and did more damage than would have been caused by the holes that would have been made in an unarmoured airscrew. Saulnier at that time fully occupied with other matters, knew nothing of my experiments. I was not even warned that the airscrew I was given was not up to flight standard but was intended only for ground-firing tests at low power.

“I had an early escape from disaster. I had just landed after a flight at 2000 metres. Immediately the engine was started centrifugal force threw off one of the bullet deflectors and the resulting unbalance of the rotating masses shook the aircraft to pieces. The wings and the fuselage were wrecked. I continued my work on the development of the device on my own. I devoted three months of research and testing to determining the best shape of airscrew and the safest form of installation, the method of tiring the gun and. above all the effectiveness of the deflectors.”

When Garros went to Saulnier he took with him his faithful mechanic Jules Hue who in translating Garros's wishes into engineering reality, did as much as create the deflector device that was adopted for operational use, as his own account relates. (This first appeared in Mortane's *Roland Garros, genie du geste et de la pensee.* and is quoted in *Roland Garros Memoirs* by Jacques Quellenee.)

"We both arrived at Villacoublay, the Morane-Saulnier aerodrome, about the end of November, I begun by picking up a sketchy mock-up that had been abandoned on a scrap-heap behind the hangars. As a starting-point it was little enough to work from, but I summoned up my courage and set to work. A corner of a hangar was put at my disposal. With the scanty resources available to me I made some deflectors and braces from some fairly thick sheet steel, a raw material that, given suitable facilities, was easy to work.

"I also made up a gun-mounting from angle-iron, the whole assembly being thoroughly primitive. Many disappointments were to beset our experiments

"We gave the first demonstration of the new device on an old Morane. Garros had just taken the aircraft to a height of 2000 m and had flown it around without firing the machine-gun He then asked me to prepare it for a firing test

"I set the aircraft up in flying position, securing it firmly. Garros arrived, checked the aircraft and got into the cockpit. I started the engine and explained some points to him: a magazine of ammunition was clipped on to the gun. Garros fired, about a dozen shots left the gun and everything collapsed. The engine fell to the ground, one blade of the airscrew having flown off and the fuselage broke behind the cockpit. What had happened? One of the braces holding the deflectors had broken, the deflector had come away and the ensuing disequilibrium had torn the engine out of its bearers. I rushed to Garros, who was unhurt: he got off with a slight shaking. I stretched out my hand to help him out of the wreckage and then the comments began. Some officers, who were present as official observers, made some sarcastic remarks aimed at me, for they did not dare to approach the great pilot . . .

"Although the test was certainly not conclusive the principle was not disproved. Next day, with Garros's full agreement and using new components, I set to work again.

"This time I made the deflectors of very hard steel of considerable thickness, and the braces were fitted to the airscrew shaft, an arrangement that gave a high degree of safety. However, when this airscrew was completed Garros decided to submit it to stringent tests at the laboratory of the *Arts et Metiers* The airscrew was put on an enormous electric motor, on which it was run for several hours at twice its normal speed The test engineer certified that the structure was immensely strong, and we left delighted

"I was allocated a new aeroplane, a Parasol for the new installation. I made a gun-mounting that was very suitable for the aircraft. It was free from vibration and the internal arrangements were much better. I also made special fittings to facilitate the changing of magazines, the discharging of empty cartridge cases, and so on. When the weapon installation was complete I tested it myself. With the engine running, some hundreds of rounds were fired without a hitch and everything worked perfectly. I continued to test and adjust the device for a few days and its success seemed so complete that Garros requested a further air-firing test before the army commission. He made this test to the considerable surprise of the members of this body. The demonstration got off to a good start with a half-hour flight and air firing.

"One unfortunate feature emerged again: the airscrew was damaged by splinters of a bullet that had shattered against a deflector, I said to Garros: 'I can get round this difficulty in a couple of days or so.'

"I dismantled the airscrew to modify its deflectors for although I had little experience in matter of this kind. I had found the key to the problem: the bullets striking the deflectors could be directed by making the deflectors channel shaped.

"Garros wasted no time. He got Chauviere to make an airscrew specially designed for the installation and Panhard to produce deflectors of the shape that our tests had proved to be the most efficient. He also had installed an 8 mm machine-gun, firing solid copper bullets that did not split up.

"For my part, I went back to Villacoublay to make some more static tests. I fired about 1000 rounds without any hitch. Garros called together a new commission of observers, made a further air-firing test, and was rewarded with a complete success. The commission could not now refuse to accept the device. At last!

"Some days passed. Suddenly, on the orders of General Headquarters we were sent post-haste to Dunkerque. We did not even have time to make any spares. The daily flights of enemy aeroplanes were striking terror into the civilian population of that sector."

It is of interest to note that Saulnier's patent depicted the braces of the deflectors as being anchored to the airscrew shaft in the manner devised by Jules Hue.

Whether by coincidence or by remarkably efficient espionage, the Germans stopped their flights over the Dunkerque area as soon as Garros arrived there. Gratified though he was to have been presented with such a challenge, Garros was also disappointed, for he felt certain that official agreement to the construction of ten aircraft armed with the deflector airscrew was imminent.

Determined to find targets for his gun, Garros patrolled the lines tirelessly until he saw three German biplanes approaching, seemingly bent on bombing Furnes He attacked several times, confident that he was shooting well at a range of only fifty metres, yet was bitterly disappointed when his shots had no visible effect. Shortly after this fruitless combat a gale swept over the aerodrome of MS.26, wrecking the *escadrille's* hangar, the falling structure of which reduced Garros's armed Type L Parasol to matchwood.

It must have been with incredulity that Garros learned, in Paris a few days later, that an official French order for more armed Type L Parasols had been cancelled when the aircraft were nearing completion. On his return lo Dunkerque Garros found that, in his absence, Jules Hue had quickly taken over a new Parasol that had been delivered a few days before the gale but had fortunately not been in the ill-fated hangar. Hue had made a new gun installation on this aircraft.

Bad weather restricted flying severely at that time, but Garros turned the inactivity to his advantage by having a bomb rack capable of carrying two 155-mm. bombs fitted to the aircraft.

After many hours of unrewarded patrolling Garros won the success he had been seeking on 1 April 1915 he had left Dunkerque with two 155-mm. bombs aboard, intent on bombing a German railway station, when he saw an enemy aircraft. He attacked, fired three magazines at the German machine and shot it down in flames. His second victory came two weeks later on 15 April when he shot down an enemy aircraft that went down in the German lines and on the 18 April an Albatros fell to his gun near Langemarck.

That afternoon Garros insisted on accompanying Capitaine de Malherbe on a bombing attack that G.H.Q. had requested. The target was Courtrai railway station Garros came down from 2000 metres to 700 metres to drop his bombs, and on his second bombing run his aircraft was hit by ground fire. The Parasol engine stopped and Garros landed near Ingel-munster. He tried to set fire to his aircraft but was only partially successful: although he evaded capture for some hours he was eventually found and made prisoner.

It has frequently been stated, quite wrongly, that Garros was flying a single-seat Morane-Saulnier Type N "Monocoque" when he was shot down. This is not so: indeed it is very doubtful whether he ever flew an aircraft of that type operationally. Ample proof that his aircraft was a Parasol is provided by the contemporary German report that appeared in the journal *Flugsport* dated 5th May 1915: When asked about his companion, he (Garros] stated, on his word of honour, that he had been the sole occupant of the aircraft and that he had been carrying two bombs in the rear seat. His motor was 80 hp only an examination of the aircraft indicated that it was a Morane monoplane and could not have carried a second person. The half-burnt aircraft including its built-in machine-gun was taken to Iseghem There was, of course no rear cockpit on the Morane-Saulnier Type N consequently the German report could relate only to a Parasol.

As Jacques Quellenec points out the German flying service benefited incalculably from Garros's capture although it had played no part in bringing down his aircraft. The weapon installation was closely studied by the Germans who despite all the nonsense printed in Fokker's so-called autobiography *Flying Dutchman,* were probably scarcely aware of its existence but immediately recognized its usefulness. From the Garros-Hue application of Raymond Saulnier's original work came the inspiration for the first operational gun-synchronizing mechanism, designed by the German engineers employed by Fokker. Ironically, the first application of the German device was made on a Fokker monoplane, which was an unabashed copy of the Morane-Saulnier Type H.

Despite the French authorities' earlier decision to cancel the initial production order for armed Type L Parasols, at least some later examples existed These may have been "homemade" conversions modified in the field but official trials of a single-seat, "Morane Parasol Fighter III," with an 80 h.p. Le Rhone engine are known to have been conducted.

J.M Bruce in correspondence with the researchers 1992

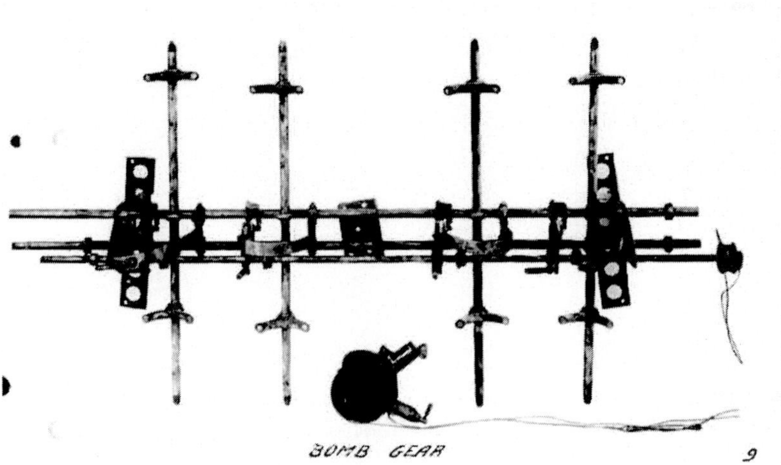

Bomb Gear

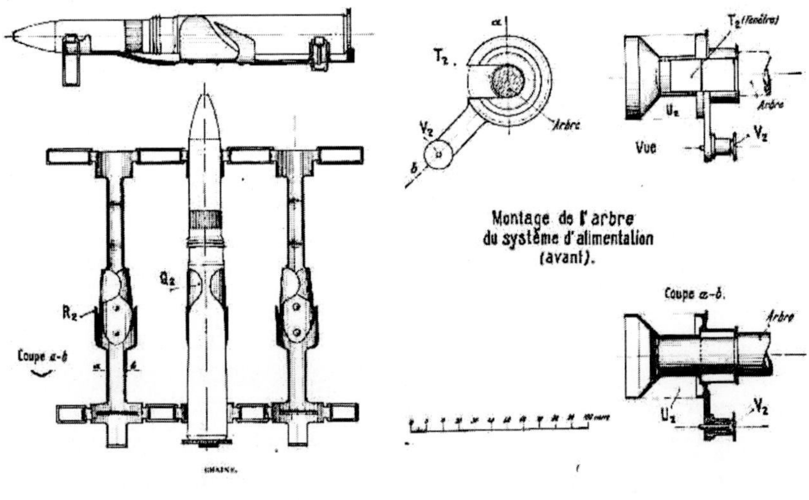

Rounds in a metal Ammunition Belt

Miscellaneous

GERMAN INFANTRY AIRCRAFT

One of the most interesting used types was the German infantry aircraft that were used towards the end of the war. During 1917 the Aircraft Manufacturers were asked to design a so-called "Infantry" airframe. This aircraft was designated with the letter J and was designed to liaise with German infantry troops and to take the battle to the Entente troops. The aircraft was intended to fly very low "in the open ground". In these conditions the pilot had little to fear from artillery shells but became vulnerable to bullets from rifles and machine guns. It was necessary to protect the airframe, the engine and the pilot and the passenger, against bullets with the appropriate armour. The armour used in the infantry aircraft programme was drawn up by the German Technical Services and was to be made of steel-nickel-chromium 5 millimetres thick, or 40 kilos' per square meter.

The aircraft had:
1 pilot;
1 passenger;
2 machine guns and ammunition;
Fuel for 3 hours of flight.
In total, 410 kilogs.

The practical ceiling imposed was 3,000 metres. The speed was to be around 140 kilometres per hour. The 200 HP Benz engine was to be used preferably for this aircraft. It was, moreover, the most widespread engine at this time of the war (1917). The solution to the design problem was given by 3 aircraft firms: Albatros, A. E. G. and Junkers. In Germany, therefore, there was great enthusiasm by the aircraft manufacturers to meet the demands of the High Command.

It should be noted that armoured aircraft had been studied in the Entente countries as well and that interesting solutions had been given. But these aircraft could not find favour with Entente pilots who, in 1917 and above all, by the end of the war, could not fly

Albatros J.1

A.E.G. J.1

Junkers J.1

ground attack aircraft because they were accustomed to flying high-altitude aircraft. Yet, many pilots flew at very low altitudes above the lines and preferred to be protected by heavy armour. Now commercial aircraft required, for reasons of economy, to have low excess power which, from the point of view of stability, would have to be of easy to fly. Perhaps it would be necessary not to lose sight of the J-type aeroplane which, if they were employed in large numbers on the battlefield, would have brought many surprises. It should not be forgotten that if wooden and canvas planes, even engine and personal were protected at vulnerable points, such as struts and guy wires, the same is not true of metal aeroplanes that when hit by bullets, can continue to fly.

The details of the load imposed on the J aircraft are as follows:

2 Crew 165 kgs

2 machine guns and ammunition 76.5 kgs

Camera 21 kgs

Fuel for 3 hours 135 kgs

Miscellaneous 12.5 kgs

Total 410 kgs

(*Entente report, translated from French*)

NOTE ON CLASSIFICATION AND DESIGNATION DIFFERENT TYPES OF GERMAN AIRCRAFT

During the war the development of aviation made the Flugzeugmeisterei lay down, in a precise manner, the rules to be followed for the classification and designation of the various types of aircraft projected or built by factories.

Classification

As early as 1915, to meet new specifications or to obtain new means of attacking enemy aircraft, the Flugzeugmeisterei demanded that the manufacturers create new types of aircraft.

The Flugzeugmeisterei left firms complete freedom in the creation of these new aircraft. (The numerical data is taken from an article by Dr. Wilh. Hoff, Director of the Deutsche Versuchsanstalt in 1920).

Designation.

To facilitate the designation of the different types of devices created by the manufacturing firms, the Flugzeugmeisterei gave each aircraft firm an abbreviated designation. Examples:
"Bay", at the Bayerische Flugzeugwerke A. G.
"Ru", at the Rumpler-Werke G. m. b. H., etc.
However, a category C aeroplane was created by the Bayerische Flugzeugwerke A. G. was called, depending on its power, Bay C I, Bay C II, etc. In 1917, increased manufacturing led to the adoption of special rules for designation for types built under licence.
Example:
An Albatros C III aircraft (Alta. C III), manufactured under licence by Bayerische Flugzeugwerke A.G., was called "Alb. C III (Bay)", the designation of the aircraft was given to the design firm with the abbreviated designation, placed in parentheses, the name of the firm which built the aircraft under license.

THE EXHIBITION OF ENEMY AIRCRAFT

20 November 1918 (Review C.G. Grey)

The public exhibition of enemy aircraft which is now open at the Agricultural Hall commends itself to the notice of everyone who is seriously interested in aviation. It comprises a really representative collection of German aeroplanes and setting aside the matter of engines, it is educative chiefly as an indication of what to avoid in aircraft design and construction.
The following machines are included among the exhibits:—
Hannoveraner two-seater fighter with 180 h.p. Opel engine
Friedrichshafen bomber with two 260 h.p. Mercedes engines
Gotha bomber with two 260 h.p. Mercedes engines
There is also the fuselage of another Gotha exhibited in section in order to reveal the famous gun tunnel.
A.E.G. bomber with two 260 h.p. Mercedes engines
Albatros two-seater
A. E.G. low-flying armoured machine.
Aviatik two-seater with 160 h.p. Benz engine.
L.V.G. two-seater with 160 h.p. Benz engine

Captured Albatros in Cairo

A.E.G. Bomber

Aviatik C.IX

Berg single seat fighter

Pfalz D.III which went to Australia

Halberstadt CL.II

L.V.G. two-seater with translucent camouflaged wings
Rumpler two-seater with 160 h.p. Mercedes engine
D.F.W. Aviatik two-seater with 160 h.p. Benz engine.
A de Havilland 9 (a British machine).
Pfalz single-seater with t6o h.p. Mercedes engine
Austrian Berg single-seater with *300* h.p Austro-Daimler engine.
Fokker single-seater triplane
Fokker single-seater biplane.
Albatros D.V single-water with 160 h.p. Mercedes engine
Albatros D. I single-seater with l60 h.p. Mercedes engine
Halberstadt single-seater with Argus engine.
Halberstadt two-seater fighter with 160 h.p. Mercedes engine

The Albatros D.V. is said to have belonged to Rittmeister Baron Manfred von Richthofen's “Circus," and the Albatros D.I was the machine on which the late Prince Friedrich Karl of Prussia was brought down.

Another Interesting exhibit is the wreckage of a "Junker" biplane, an all-metal machine with a Benz engine. This aeroplane seems to be the result of an aerial nightmare, and a determination to construct an all-metal machine at all costs. The most Interesting feature is the wing construction. The wing is extraordinarily deep in section and is built up on eight tubular aluminium main spars, arranged in two rows of four and cross- braced with aluminium tubing. The minor members of the framework are constructed of sheet metal and the wing covering consists of painted corrugated aluminium sheets. In its undamaged condition the machine must have looked like a huge model of a German made toy of the type which used to be made in this country at 6½ d .

One imagines that the vibration of these wings of metal would make the machine very unpleasant to fly, especially in the event of uneven firing of the engine.

A little grim humour is displayed in a tableau representing a crashed Albatros single seater after “a fall from 6000 feet." The greatest pains have been taken to lend realism to this exhibit and every detail has been faithfully supplied—not forgetting the corpse

As a rule, the engines have been removed from the machines for test but a representative collection of enemy engines, complete and dissected, is shown, including Mercedes, Benz, Argus, Austro-Daimler, German le Rhone and Oberursel types.

Aeroplane instruments and equipment of all kinds are also on view and the walls are adorned with numerous instruction, pictures from British flying schools showing the budding pilot what to do, what not to do and what will happen if he does what he should not.

The exhibition is open to the public from 10 a.m. to 8 p.m. on Monday, Wednesday, Thursday and Saturday of each week only. Admission is 1/-, the proceeds going to charity and for the twofold purpose the money is well spent.

Captured Albatross D.V on display

Captured enemy aircraft exhibition St James Park, London

OBSERVATION BALLOONS

THE BALLOON SERVICE

The kite balloons which were built by von Parseval and von Sigsfeld in 1896 were introduced into the German Army to take the place of the spherical captive balloon. With the appearance of the aeroplane interest in the spherical observation balloon waned. The German army assumed that the aeroplane would soon replace the balloon for observation service. When war broke out in 1914 and war became stationary due to trench warfare the balloon rendered valuable service by locating hostile artillery, supply columns and movement of enemy troops. Very soon there arose the demand for an improved type of balloon. The balloon of 21000 cubic feet capacity, which theoretically was supposed to ascend to 2500 feet, in practice would never rise above 1600 feet whenever there was a slight wind blowing. This was not high enough to maintain an efficient watch over enemy artillery, particularly as the enemy soon began to take the observation balloon into consideration when selecting their bombarding positions. In order to attain greater heights many of the appliances that were fitted to the heavy basket were removed; in fact, the observers resorted to the flimsiest of mounts a kind of stiff saddle slung beneath the envelope or some similar arrangement.

The personnel of the balloon service itself were composed almost entirely of volunteers and skilled mechanics that were well drilled and trained and of excellent quality. The officers were recruited from every branch of the service and highly efficient officers: some of whom had been trained at the Staff College and were finished off by a one-year's course at the Airship Training School. In addition to that, twenty officers every year underwent a four months' course to qualify them as balloon observers with the Airship Defence Corps.

Balloon officers had to be acquainted with the following subjects: a knowledge of the properties and use of gas, the science of free ballooning, experience in defence against aeroplane attack, the proper use of anti-aircraft quick-firing guns and machine guns; practice in the use of field glasses from a swaying balloon basket and experience

Drachen Observation Balloon being deployed in Flanders March 1915

in guiding troops during an attack so as to be able to undertake operations with the infantry and similar work.

Beginning in early 1915, balloons of 28000 and 35000 cubic feet capacity were sent to the Western front. These balloons could ascend to 3300 or 4000 feet and as they did not rock so badly in the wind it was easier to observe from them. Due to heavy demands on manpower the party of soldiers, used to pull the balloon down were replaced by a horse towing a trolley. This impacted on the balloons tactical handling till the mechanical winch was introduced. Due to their usefulness the number of balloon tasks was increased especially with heavy artillery. At the end of 1915 there were more than forty balloon units on active service on the Western front. Due to the increase of aeroplane attacks, it became necessary to accelerate the descent of the balloons and motor winches of 24 hp or even 50 and 60 hp were employed.

The greatest improvement that was made, however, consisted of a new type of balloon. On the Somme Front the Entente produced a new pattern of balloon; the Germans had succeeded in capturing one of these balloons- the Cacquot. It was copied but slightly altered and was produced under the name of the A.E. balloon. This balloon was oblong in shape, of 30000 c.f. capacity, and was provided with air-filled ballonets instead of planes for the purpose of stability. This balloon remained almost motionless in the air, instead of rolling to 30 degrees as the old type used to do. It did not drift so far to leeward, could attain a height of 5000 feet, was very steady and could even ascend with a wind velocity of 65 feet/sec., whereas the 'Drachen' the old type, was useless for observation purposes in a wind velocity of only 45 feet/sec.

Later type of observation balloon the A.E. balloon ready to ascend

Natural rubber, which was so important for the manufacture of balloon fabric, soon became so scarce that synthetic and waste rubber had to be used as a substitute. Eventually rubber was given up altogether and the balloons were made of doped fabric and in the final types gut membrane was inserted between the inner and outer layers of the balloon envelope. One of the suppliers of fabric was the Balloon Fabric Co. at Augsburg

The Balloon Service of the German Army was one branch of the Air Service and was supervised by one section at the Air Service Headquarters. The Balloon Section at these Headquarters had charge of the organization of balloon units in the field and at home, new formations, demobilisation and modification of instructions, personnel, technical matters and replacement of material in the Balloon Service and in balloon barrage sections. At the Army Air Service Headquarters, one second lieutenant had charge of balloon panoramas, preparation and exploitation of balloon photographs and the training of balloon observers in photography. It appeared that the Army Air Service Headquarters was chiefly interested in the information that could be obtained from balloon photographs and limited its activity to the development of this work.

The Balloon Service played an important part in the Army area; it may be assumed that the direction of all other work done by balloon units was left to other branches of the service, of which artillery was probably the most important. The small amount of influence which the Army Air Service headquarters had over the Balloon Service may also be explained by the fact that a staff officer at the headquarters of each Group of Armies had charge of all balloon detachments in the Groups and allotted them to the various parts of the Group front, according to the amount of activity.

On the most active parts of the Western Front, a detachment was allotted to each division and received its orders from that division. According to an order captured from the 1st German Army, dated 15 April 1917, a section of balloons served permanently in each division for artillery observation and was subject to the orders of the Commander of the Divisional Artillery. All balloons in excess of the requirements of the divisional artillery would be held for special work, such as long observation, or were distributed to the divisions. In each group area, all balloons except those assigned to divisional artillery, were under the orders of the detachment commander. The balloon section (Ballonzug) was the tactical unit and consisted of two balloons, one for front line duty and one in reserve. While the organisation allotted two balloons to a section. It is doubtful whether units had their full quota at the time the Armistice was signed, because there appeared to be a shortage of balloons. The section was commanded by a captain or lieutenant and had three or four officer-observers (lieutenants) who usually had been trained in artillery work. The personnel consisted of approximately 120 men, 10 of whom were non-commissioned officers. Soldiers seldom made ascensions in the balloon. The section was equipped with a winch, a truck, and several wagons. The winding gear consisted of the winch and a motor, mounted on separate vehicles, which were coupled together when the balloon was up and could be separated when the section was moving. Balloons were concealed by camouflage paint while in their beds and were given a few small cannon and machine guns for protection against Entente aircraft. Each observer was equipped with a parachute.

As a rule there was only one observer in the balloon basket and it was only during training that two were sent up simultaneously. To make better use of the balloons without increasing their number, experiments were carried out in 1917 with two baskets slung beneath one envelope;a method which, even at the front, gave satisfactory results up to a height of about 3000 feet. This practice was, however, soon abandoned, for the two baskets upset the stability of the balloon and caused violent rocking.

An observer fires a signal flare from a balloon gondola

A captured document showed that the balloon sections in each Corps were organised in a battle group known as Balloon-Kampf-Gruppe, which received its orders directly from the Corps headquarters. Balloon sections were grouped into balloon

Observation balloon on the march

Captive balloon train stuck in the mud

detachments (Feldluftschiffen Abteilungen) which usually had their headquarters with those of the Corps. The detachment appeared to have been a flexible unit that increased and decreased in size with the importance of the sector. It was not assigned to a Corps but to a certain sector and operated with the Corps located in that sector. It received its orders from the officer in charge of balloons at the headquarters of the group of Armies through the Army headquarters. In addition to the various sections in the detachment, the staff of the detachment, the staff of the detachment consisted of a commanding officer (captain) and adjutant (lieutenant) in charge of office work another lieutenant, who had charge of maps and photographs and about thirty soldiers who were employed in the orderly room, photographic section, map section, signal section and as drivers, cooks and canteen men. Both balloon section and detachments were numbered from one upwards but inasmuch as a section was often transferred from one detachment to another, it was impossible to identify one through the other. It had been reported that there was an Army Balloon Commander who had charge of all balloon units in the Army area and the Army balloon park, who was under the direction of the General staff of the Army. In addition to these duties, he was responsible for:-

1. Advising the Army Staff in all matters affecting balloons and forwarding all reports of tactical importance to the Staff.
2. Keeping in touch with the Intelligence Section (report centre) of the Staff of the Artillery General at Array Headquarters.
3. Arranging for the protection of balloons.
4. Exchanging the results of reconnaissance with neighbouring Armies.
5. Supervising the work of balloons detachments.

If this condition existed it was of comparatively recent organisation (autumn 1918), because the organisation of the 4th German Army at the beginning of 1918 did not provide for an officer of this sort. It had also been reported that the Service of Supply was under the Inspektion der Luftschiffertruppen, which was located in Berlin. If this was correct, the Inspektion der Luftschiffertruppen supplied material as directed by Air Service headquarters, because the organization of the Air Service Headquarters provided for the supply and replacement of material. Supplies were procured through the Army Balloon Park. According to the statement of a prisoner, the gas necessary for balloons on the western front, was made in the Etterbreek factory at Brussels and were supplied with gas from Kovno. The gas was sent to the sections by train under the supervision of a conveyor (Bellistman) belonging to the section. In addition there were a certain number of units called Gas Kollonnen, which apparently conveyed gas tanks from the Army Balloon Park to the Balloon sections. Damaged balloons were packed into a railway truck,

Deploying the balloon envelope before inflation

Observers ready to ascend 27 July 1916

Ready to ascend with a 120 cm focal distance camera

one man was detailed to accompany the truck to Reinickendorf, returning with a new balloon. This trip usually took a week. If a section had no reserve balloon to use in this case, it borrowed one from a neighbouring section. The winches were manufactured by the Augsburger Machinenfabrik, and the repair depot was at Cologne in an old Zeppelin hangars. A prisoner, captured in the autumn of 1917, stated that there were five replacement depots at that time, each with a training battalion from which men were sent on requisition to the Army Balloon Parks and from there to their sections. It was also stated that these battalions were located as follows:-

Reinickendorf - First Battalion
Darmstadt - Second Battalion
Duren - Third Battalion
Mannheim - Fourth Battalion
Liegnitz - Fifth Battalion

There was no later Information available concerning the methods of training and replacing balloon personnel but the Balloon Service has not grown to any extent since then and it appears that the system has neither been changed nor enlarged.

<u>Balloon Communication</u>

The Balloon was connected by telephone to a ground station near the balloon winch. Messages were taken by one operator and passed to another who worked on a line connecting the ground station with the Balloon Central Station. The latter was connected by telephone to the detachment headquarters, division headquarters, divisional artillery commander and the heavy artillery commander. All messages were sorted at this filter station and sent to the proper parties. The number of Central Balloon Stations in a sector depended on the number of balloon detachments there. All balloon detachments were also connected through central exchanges with the staff officer at the Army Group Headquarters. During a hostile attack on a large scale, the detachment staffs were responsible for observing the progress of the attack and forwarding this information to all staffs concerned. Every evening each balloon detachment made up and circulated by telephone a comprehensive report of balloon observations during the day. Balloons were usually employed for the following work:-

A. Artillery observation.
B. Infantry observation
C. Balloon barrages.

A. Artillery observation: The following information, taken from a captured document, dated 13 July 1918 (French Second Army Bulletin 22-9-18) shows the manner in which artillery balloons were employed. A group consisting of several batteries was formed, and allotted one balloon. The work of the group was directed and supervised by the artillery commander and the targets to be fired upon were chosen by the balloon observer, the batteries having authority to fire on any target chosen by him. The point emphasised in the order is that all targets should be picked up quickly, especially moving targets.

B. Infantry balloon: In order to establish communication with the infantry in the front line, some divisions had captive balloons allotted to them which were employed as "Infantry Balloons". As they enabled observation to be carried out for a long period from the same spot and reports to be transmitted direct by telephone, they were particularly well suited for keeping a look-out over the battlcfield. Their employment, however, was largely dependent on weather conditions. The infantry balloon carried a conical pennant on its basket and accepted signals as long as the pennant was flying. The observer was connected by telephone with a ground station.

Communication between the observer and the front line was also carried out by means of wireless and lamp signalling apparatus. The wireless ground stations were taken from divisional wireless detachments, formed a part of the system of these detachments, and were manned and operated by them. Endeavours were made to allot a wireless station to at least one balloon in each divisional sector. Wireless stations, however, were to be used only in case the telephone connections to the various command posts were cut off, or if, owing to the number of balloons having been increased suddenly, it was impossible to have the telephone lines laid. The signals sent by lamp were identified with the wireless signals laid down for infantry airplanes in the "Signal Code". At night, the Infantry balloon worked like an ordinary lamp signalling station and frequently sent out flashed to facilitate the aiming of flashes in its direction.

C. Balloon barrages: Balloons were used for this purpose only in exceptional cases, such as protecting an important factory from raids by Entente bombing machines. A prisoner, captured in June, 1918, stated that balloon barrages were used only around important centres near the front, such as Ronbach and Hagendingen and that in spite of these balloon barrages, the planes were subject to aerial attack. The heavy losses of German balloons brought about a more conservative system of employing them. Following is a translation of a captured German order covering this point.

1. The heavy losses in balloons and balloon material require that balloons should be used with discretion.

2. In case of a fog or high wind Balloon Section No.24 will send up a balloon to report on the conditions for observation. The section commander will then judge if balloons should be sent up. Balloons must only be sent up in unfavourable weather when the fighting requires it.

3. During periods of rest, artillery officers will make balloon ascents so as to become accustomed to the work and duties of observation and also to the methods employed.

4. Balloon stations as far as possible must not be in the vicinity of any camp or road frequented by troops.

For Staff Major, (Signed) *VON DEM HAGEN.*

The following are a few general principles observed from the Entente side of the line on the tactical employment of German balloons:-

1. An Increase in the number of balloons was apt to take place a few days before an attack. It was very difficult for an observer to do good work in a country that was entirely new to him. To obviate this, he was frequently allowed to make an ascent from the emplacement he was to use on the day of the attack for a brief survey of the terrain.

2. It quite frequently happened in quiet sectors that one balloon was used in two or three different emplacements several kilometres apart on the same day. The emplacements used were usually near good roads and with a winch capable of making twelve miles an hour, these moves were not difficult to accomplish. It necessitated, however, a careful recording of the time at which a balloon was in ascension at a certain emplacement in order to note any increase in

Inside a gondola

Jumping while under attack

the total number of balloons in use. Such an Increase was a possible indication of an attack, or reinforcement preliminary to an attack.

3. In the sector of an American division It was noted that:-

a. Only three of the balloons had fixed bases but these in descending, passed from view while still at a considerable height.

b. Eight of the visible balloons were mobile and frequently changed their positions in the air as much as two kilometres.

c. The balloons operated in a cone 8-10 kilometres from our front lines. It has been more difficult to identify German balloon units than flights because of the few prisoners captured from the Balloon Service and because of the unfamiliarity of officers and men in other branches of the service with the balloon organisation.

It has been impossible to obtain information which would give the detachment to which each section was assigned because the sections were transferred from one detachment to another as tactical needs required. Inasmuch as balloon sections were numbered from one upwards. It appears that all units were not identified. The number of German balloon sections, as identified on 11 November 1918 was numbered up to 312 and included Bavarian and Saxon units.

Following is a November report from British Intelligence on the deployment of balloons for passive defence:-
"From recent reports it appears that the defence of some individual factories by a Balloon barrage (Luftsperr) is carried out on the following lines:-
Balloons are let up at intervals of 400 yards in a rough circle round the objective to be defended, the radius of the circle varying with the size of the factory. Thus, at Oppau, the chemical works are defended by balloons situated in a circle, with a radius of 1,500 yards from the centre of the works. The average height of the balloons appeared to be about 4000 to 5000 feet but pilots report having sighted a balloon barrage at a height of 6000 to 8000 feet.

In addition to the cable connecting the balloon with the winch, a supplementary cable, fastened to the ground some distance from the winch is used to keep the balloon steady. Horizontal wires connect adjacent balloons and it is believed that vertical wires are suspended from these horizontal wires forming a species of net. The horizontal wires are electrified though the object of this electrification is not apparent. One report states that the power station of the Bayer's chemical works at Leverkusen is provided with an aerial about 450 feet high from the top of which electric cables lead the current to the nacelle of each balloon. Notices have also appeared in the Mannheim Press warning the population not to touch any of the wires used in connection with the balloon barrage, as they are charged with a strong electric current.

In actual practice such barrages have not proved a serious hindrance to bombing operations. The maximum height is not usually sufficient to prevent accurate results being obtained. It is, however, important to pass to the squadrons all information available relative to these barrages, since it may well affect the altitude at which raids are carried out over objectives so protected."

Kite Balloons

(Details from Entente inspections)

Firms associated with their manufacture: -

A. Spindler & Hoyer G. m. b. H. - Balloon Sextants-Gottingen, Kônigsallee 23

1. Ballonhüllen G. m.'b. H. Tempelhof Field Balloons
2. O. Jungnickel Reinickendorf, Scharnweberstr 6 -Balloon Baskets
3. Luftfahrzeug G. m. b. H. Bitterfeld Field Balloons
4. Riedinger A.-G. Augsburg Field Balloons, Balloon baskets
5. E. Schlesinger & Co. Wilmersdorf, Aschaffenburger Str. 8 - Balloon baskets
6. Vereinigte Gummiwarenfabriken Marburg on Elbe. Field Balloons

Balloon Sheds

1. F. Behrens & A. Kühne Oschersleben
2. Fabrik für Eisenhochb-u Bracken-Louis Eilers Hanover Herrenhausen
3. Otto Hetzner A.-G. Weimar

GAS DEPOTS (FORMERLY MILITARY)

1. Darmstadt
2. Dresden
3. Düsseldorf-Lohausen
4. Janbol
5. Jüterbog
6. Kônigsberg
7. Mannheim
8. Reinickendorl
9. Schneidemühl

Captured Balloon Materials (Entente Inspections)

Two Captive balloon baskets, three balloon valves

11th July -17th July-Decision received from Paris that kite balloon material was the property of the Allies. Its destruction organised.

25th September-Large number of kite balloon winches found at Stuttgart.

23 June 1920-The observation balloons, winches, balloon cabling, and all other material appertaining to them, unquestionably come within the meaning of Article 202, and should be delivered by the German Government to the I. A. A. C. C.

Observation balloon material not having been included in the nomenclature of Article 202 of the Peace Treaty, the Germans

An observation balloon bedded down at Coblenz, December 1919

declared that this material should not be included as aeronautical material. It was not until 7 July 1920 that this question was settled in a decisive manner. The delivery and the destruction of this material has necessarily suffered a considerable delay.

January 1921-During the past fortnight the following material has been discovered by the I. A. A. C. C.:-

1 aeroplane, 127 engines, 140 cases of engine spares, a large number of magnetos, 68 propellers, 150 cases of wireless material, 7 kite balloon envelopes, 6 canvas hangars.

The following material has been declared by the R. T. G., 10 aeroplanes, 42 engines, 61 cases of spares, 29 magnetos, 12 cameras, and 216 cases of various instruments.

AIRCRAFT MATERIAL INSPECTION AND TESTING

Materials:-. The following Information concerning the supply of material used in the construction of aeroplanes was obtained from a prisoner captured in June, 1918. Since then there has been even a more marked shortage, which the German Air Service has attempted to remedy by using substitute materials.

1. Wood. Timber used in aircraft construction has been artificially dried because the old stock of naturally dried wood had been almost exhausted. The use of this wood, which was very sensitive to any change of weather, led to a warping of the wings and consequently to a decrease in the life of machines at the front. It had also caused a

great shortage of propellers. The quality of timber used for aircraft construction had deteriorated considerably. Walnut was scarce and all existing supplies and even trees were takes charge of by Military authorities.

2. Rubber. The extreme shortage of this material could not be exaggerated and up to June, 1918, German Industry had been unable to produce a substitute satisfactory in either quality or quantity. Rubber supports for the radiators were very bad; shook absorbers on undercarriages were steel springs and occasionally compressed air was used for this purpose; hollow wooden wheels were frequently used on training aircraft. Rubber washers on the water pipes of motors, etc., were often of poor quality. The prisoners also stated that many forced landings could be attributed to the poor quality of the rubber used. Inasmuch as a good substitute for hard rubber had been found, the Air Service did not feel the absence of this product.

3. Copper and brass. There was a distinct shortage of copper and brass and as a result of this shortage all supplies of these commodities, such as domestic utensils, door fittings, handles on railway carriages etc., were confiscated, no distinction being made between Government and private property. Petrol tanks and pipes were no longer made of brass, but of sine-lined iron sheeting. Benz aluminium and Mercedes Argus iron were used as substitutes for copper in the construction of conduction pipes of motors.

4. Aluminium. It appears that this article was also scarce because existing supplies were confiscated and practically no aluminium was used in the interior

5. Iron and steel. No shortage

6. Paint and varnish were of poor quality and of insufficient quantity.

7. Oil. The shortage of oil had not been felt in the Air Service by June, 1918, as it had in other branches of the service. The quality was still satisfactory at that time.

8. Linen was still exclusively used for wing covering but it had deteriorated in quality.

9. Cellon dope. Both quality and quantity were still satisfactory in June, 1918.

10. Glue was scarce and of poor quality.

11. Grease had deteriorated considerably.
12. Dyes were of poor quality and the quantity available was Insufficient.

B. Inspection and Testing. The following Information on Inspection and testing was obtained from two prisoners, captured in June 1918. The information given by these prisoners has been found reliable in all cases. All orders for machines and accessories were transmitted through the Flugzeugmeisterei der Inspection der Fliegertruppen at Charlottenburg. The control of construction and acceptance was carried out by the Zentrale Abnahme Kommission, which consisted of technically trained officers, N.C.O's and men. All parts of an aircraft which were subject to any strain were examined by the Zentrale Abnahme Kommission for instance struts, spars, finished wings, turnbuckles and bracing wires were tested under compression and tension.

A number of engineers and technically trained personnel represented the Government at each factory having contracts for the Army or Navy, in order to guarantee the use of suitable material. It was not always possible to carry out the regulations of the Zentrale Abnahme Kommission as the available controlling personnel were not always sufficient to cope with the volume of production. It should also be remembered that there was a certain amount of corruption among the employees of the Zentrale Abnahme Kommission.

A percentage of each series was examined by the Prufanstalt und Werft. One machine of each type was sent to the Prufanastalt und Werft for wing testing. The machine was turned upside down and a load of sand was gradually applied on the wings up to the breaking point. The factor of safety, which was 6 before 1916, had been reduced by 1918. It was reported that the factor of safety of the new L.V.Q. C.V. was 3.7.

Machines of every type, before being handed over to the Government, had to be flown with full load. The prisoners were unable to give exact figures on these tests, as they varied according to the type but every machine had to attain an altitude of at least 8000 metres and to pass an endurance test of one hour. In bad weather the flying tests were modified considerably. Test pilots at the factories were always civilians and drew very high salaries. After the flying test had satisfactorily been carried out by the civilian pilot, the machine was again tested by a military pilot belonging to the Zentrale Abnahme Commission. In case the latter was not satisfied with the aeroplane, it was returned to the factory. Zentrale Abnahme Kommission pilots appeared to be fairly susceptible to bribes.

After having been passed by the Zentrale Abnahme Kommission aeroplane destined for the front were sent to the army aircraft parks, and school aeroplanes were sent to the Flieger Ersatz Abteilungen (training squadrons). There was only a small depot with the Prufanstalt und werft. Aeroplanes were sent to the army aircraft parks fully equipped, with the exception of Instruments.

Each new engine was subjected to a 24-hour test at the factory, under the supervision of the Zentrale Abnahme Kommission. The motor was then dismantled and each part examined. Faulty parts were replaced end the engine had to undergo another short trial. Cylinders and pistons were tested under hydraulic pressure before the motor was assembled. Apart from a very small proportion which went to the parks, all motors were sent to the aircraft factories, where they were built into machines, engines, fixed machine guns, bomb-dropping gear and wireless telegraph apparatus were built at the factory. The installation of the wireless telegraph apparatus was carried out by military employees of the F.T. Rust Kommando at Berlin, who were attached for duty with the various firms. The bomb dropping gear was frequently altered and reconstructed by units at the front. Instruments were stored at the depots of the various units and were mounted at the front.

Only small repairs were carried out by units at the front for example, the replacements of under-carriages, rudders and elevators and small repairs on the wings. Aeroplanes which had to undergo important repairs were sent to the Prufanstalt und Werft. The more important repairs on motors were also under-taken by the Prufanstalt und Werft, who returned the motor to the factory if they were unable to make the necessary repairs. A test of three hours was imposed after the repairs had been completed. Motors of the Mercedes Benz and Argus types were usually overhauled after sixty flying hours, even though no faults had become apparent. The overhauling was done thoroughly at a Flieger Ersatz Abteilung, but somewhat superficially by the units at the front. Mercedes motors, which were known to have a long life, were usually sent to the Prufanstalt und Werft for thorough examination after having been overhauled four times.

It was the practice of firms not to accumulate a stock of motors but to work on current orders only. The number of spare motors at each park was relatively small as compared with the number of aircraft with the Army, i.e., 1 to 20. With the exception of R. Abteilungen, units at the front did not carry a stock of spare engines. Jagdstaffeln (fighter flights) usually had two or three spare aeroplanes, other units were supposed to have one spare aircraft each, but often did not have this allotment. With the exception of the R. Abteilungen, units at the front carried very few spare parts with them. They did, however, have at least one spare propeller per aeroplane.

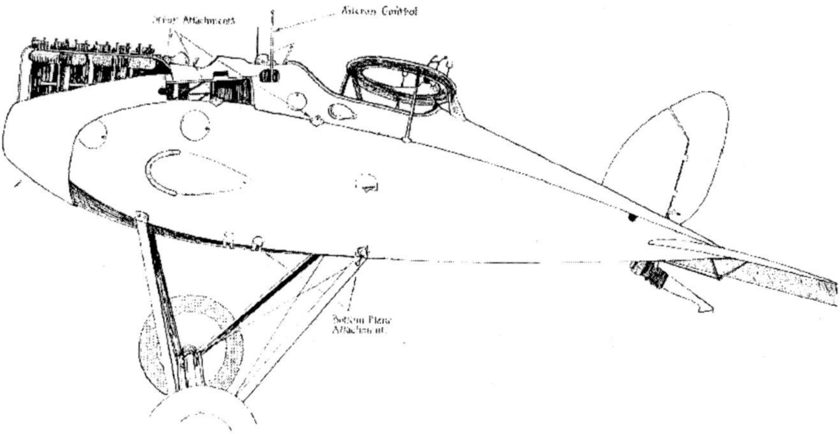

Halberstadt two seater

Aeroplanes and seaplanes delivered to the Entente by 16 April 1921

TYPE	GREAT BRITAIN	FRANCE	ITALY	BELGIUM	JAPAN	TOTAL
Albatros.	8	16	9	5	11	49
A. E. G..	1	2	—	—	1	4
Brandenburg	7	3	7	12	11	40
D. F. W.	7	15	1	6	8	37
F. D. H. (Friedrichshafener) ..	8	10	11	15	9	53
Fokker	9	12	17	19	9	66
Gotha	8	9	5	1	7	30
Halberstadt.	2	3	8	2	4	19
Hannover.	—	—	1	1	1	3
Junker	4	5	7	3	7	26
L. V. G..	11	11	18	17	6	63
Pfalz..	11	19	11	7	7	55
Rubild.	6	6	6	4	3	25
Rumpler	6	7	4	19	3	39
Roland	4	4	11	3	3	25
Siemens Schuckert..	4	4	5	2	5	20
Other Types	8	11	6	1	5	31
TOTAL...	104	137	127	117	100	585

WAR MATERIAL

The proportional distribution of material surrendered under Article 202 of the Peace Treaty was based upon the distribution of war booty captured at the Armistice and was as follows:-

Great Britain	30%
France	30%
Italy	15 %
Japan	15%
U.S.A	15%
Belgium	5%

NOTE: - The 30% allocated to Great Britain includes any materials required by, or destined for, the British dominions. Due to the failure of the American Government to ratify the Peace Treaty, the proportion of material originally allocated to U.S. was divided in equal proportions amongst Italy, Japan and Belgium. The final percentages as a basis of distribution were therefore as follows:

Great Britain	30%
France	30 %
Italy	20%
Japan	10%
Belgium	10 %

Captured Pfalz D.III

LIST (Aeroplanes)

List of German aeroplanes not required for distribution amongst Entente and Associated Powers and which can in consequence be rendered unfit for further use, without further orders.

Albatros...	B.2	Fokker…	D.2	LVG…	B.3
	B.2a		D.3		C.1
	C.2		D.5		C.2
	C.3		D.6		C.3
	C.4	Gotha…	G.1		C.4
	C.6		G.2		D.3
	C.7		G.3	Pfalz…	C.1
	C.10		G.4		D.3
	D.1	Halberstadt…	C.2		D.3a
	D.2		C.5		D.5
	D.3		C.L.2		D.7
	D.7		C.L.4	Roland…	C.10
A.E.G.…	B.42		C.L.5		D.2
	C.1		C.L.S.1	Rumpler…	B.1
	C.2	Hannoveraner…	C.1		C.1
	C.4		C.2		C.1a
Aviatik …	C.1		C.6		C.2
	C.2		C.11		C.3
	C.3		C.IVa		C.4
A.G.O....	‘’		C.L.2		C.5
A.W.S…	D.5		C.L.3a		D.1
D.F.W…	C.4		C.L.5	M.A.N…	C.L.2
	D.1	L.V.G….	B.2		
Fokker…	D.R.1		B.2a		
	D.1				
	D.2				

Coblenz Airfield

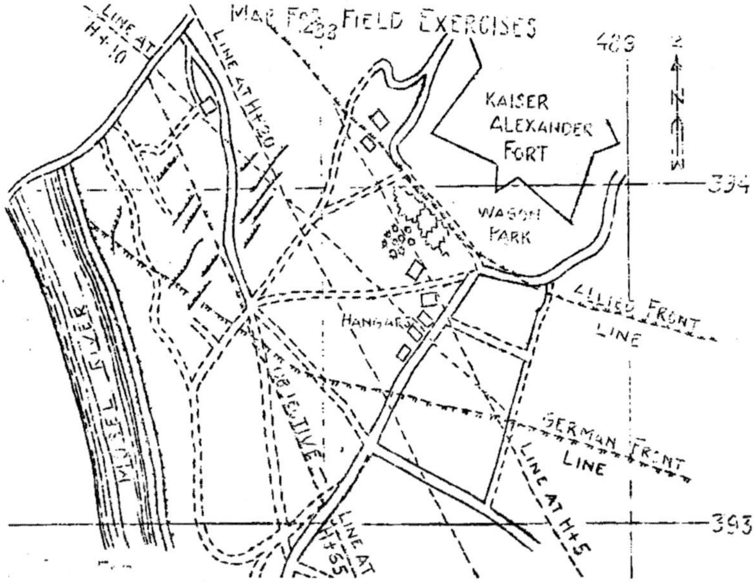

Allocation of German Aeroplanes
Entente Forces Coblenz
2 January 1919

Fifty Fokker D.VII (F) part of fifty of the 4th Shipment arrived by railroad (RR) from various places.

Plane Number	Engine Number	RR Car number
10348	Mana 53	48608 Breslau
7799	BMW 1679	47779 Breslau
Above designed for flight but lost in RR yards		
7772	BMW 12132	25054 Els-Loth
7744	BMW 1560	33079 Elberfeld
7800	Mercedes 46557	46618 Halle
7761	BMW 1633	41777 Halle
7795	BMW 1670	44125 Berlin
7776	Mercedes 45778	44354 Halle
7752	Mercedes 45771	45711 Halle
7802	Mercedes 45685	43790 Berlin
7732	BMW 12087	83725 Magdeburg
7788	BMW 1674	104331 Essen
7768	BMW 1622	82624 Magdeburg
7794	BMW 1675	24524 Brom
7789	Mercedes 45704	41962 Halle
7747	BMW 12096	43892 Berlin
7781	BMW 1668	26817 Coln
7730	BMW 1608	20414 Halle
7770	BMW 1619	103360 Essen
7605	Mercedes 36966	28063 Coln
7783	BMW 1635	104631 Essen
7796	BMW 12141	80232 Magdeburg
7775	Mercedes 45795	46095 Burtteburg
4292	Mana 12	43372 Halle
10350	Mercedes 45659	44697 Halle
7729	BMW 1626	28034 Coln
7740	BMW 1575	83080 Magdeburg
8476	BMW 1583	47012

Plane Number	Engine Number	RR Car number
10347	Mana 23	79945 Nurnburg
5138	Mercedes 34561	30938 Coln
7753	Mercedes 45651	27366 Coln
7766	Mercedes 45632	82989 Magdeburg
7786	BMW 1671	77122 Munchen
7762	BMW 1634	28082 Coln
7797	BMW 12144	47606 Breslau
10349	Mercedes 45700	26100 Erfurt
7803	Mercedes 45673	26911 Saarbruck
7790	Mercedes 45876	46579 Halle
7777	Mercedes 45658	80171 Magdeburg
7785	BMW 1644	46691 Halle

Note: Manifest had heavy blurring on original letters and digits, 7781 had no propeller, 7775 had two propellers, 7777 and 7785 selected for flight.

German Aeroplanes at Treves Aerodrome allocated to the United States for test and study:-

Type	Number
Pfalz DXII	2630 and 2598
DFW C.V	6763 and 4317/18
Halberstadt C.L. II	4317/18 and 1253/18
Halberstadt C.L. IV	5840/18 and 5817/18
Halberstadt C.V	6681/18 and 8727/18
AEG	350/18
AEG G.II	353/18
AEG G	572/18
LVG C VI	8980 and 1740
Rumpler Rubild Mb	4023/18
Rumpler Ru.C.IV	4067/18
Hanover C.L. IIIA	13339/18
Hanover C. L.	13321

8487/18

Two D.VII's at Coblenz

Fokker D.VIIs awaiting disposal

Fokker D.VII 7755/18 and others awaiting disposal

Fokker D.VII 8425/18

P108 Fokker D.VII 7776/18

United States Army Fokker D.VII A58530

United States Army Fokker D.VII 8403

Fokker D.VII 7788/18

Fokker D.VII (GAW) to be accepted by the United States Coblenz 30 January 1919

Plane number	RR Car Number	Plane Number	RR Car number
8357	51425	8632	42883
8349	81231	8593	42883
8336	45016	8456	45016
8392	44254	8519	33199
8525	27802	8538	33199
8553	27802	8503	42723
8403	41651	8543	30344
8396	41651	8338	103454
8550	104395	8316	83499
8322	45828	8542	83499
8609	26749	8507	42293
8589	26749	8331	42993
8567	46526		
8549	42782		
8502	42782		
8526	720033		
8520	82280		
8414 (Flown)	46133		

Fokker D.VII (F) to be accepted by the United States
(All equipment including compass and twin machine guns were mounted)

Aircraft Serial	Car number
7757	20395
7782	26905
7780	48915
7763	104602
7765	81325
7773	(48003) Flown tested in Flight
5074	19707
7767	59889
7774	32655
5100	4538

Fokker D.VII 7756/18

Fokker D.VII 7788/18

Fokker D.VII 7744/18

Fokker D.VII 8541/18

Fokker D.VII 10348

Fokker D.VII 8331/18

Fokker D.VII 7795/18

Fokker D.VII 8414/18

Fokker D.VII under United States guard 1919

An upper wing transferred to the United States

Fokker D.VII 8539/18

Fokker D.VII 8508/18

Aircraft spare parts being delivered to the American Air Service

Fokker D.VII aircraft wing under guard

Swiss Air Force Fokker D.VII 621

Coblenz 1 January 1919
Aeroplanes accepted from the German Commission
(For the United States)

Plane number	Engine number	RR Car
8425	Mercedes 44996	Tested in flight
8489	BMW 12072	Tested in flight
8530	Mercedes 45158	104108
8508	Mercedes 32779	104108
8540	Mercedes 35554	80315
8518	BMW 1578	77298
8330	Mercedes 36164	54707
8351	Mercedes 44975	54707
8541	Mercedes 45148	83151
8342	Mercedes 37526	83151
6412	Mercedes 44220	33209
8323	Mercedes 40715	33209
8345	Mercedes 45590	33209
8583	Mercedes 42527	46749
8517	Mercedes 43537	82212
8528	Mercedes 45920	83594
8470	BMW 1453	70244
8501	BMW 1502	70244
8539	Mercedes 45056	70244

NOTE: Fokker 8489, 6412, 8583, 8528 have no compass mounted on them. A sufficient number of compasses to make up this deficiency are included in the RR car of spare parts. Fokker 8425, 6412, 8345 have two guns mounted on each. The guns for all the other planes of this list were found in the car of spare parts.

Fokker D.VII (F)

Plane number	Engine number	RR Car
7756	Mercedes 41152	24671
7755	BMW 11618	83479
7781	Mercedes 32109	42023
7788	BMW 1656	30640
7864	BMW 1630	47071
7784	BMW 1669	45616
7798	BMW 12102	80723
5088	Mercedes 43327	42524
7771	BMW 1621	43441
7792	Mercedes 45790	48034
7787	BMW 1667	56719

Note: All these planes are equipped with instruments and guns.

Roland D.VI (B) (Coblenz 1 January 1919)

6141	Benz	29205	Tested in flight crashed on landing
7518	Benz	29218	48668
7504	Benz	29176	20771
3617	via Mercedes	42164	41716
2265	Benz	29077	119651
3632	via Mercedes	33921	76716
6123	Benz	29053	41485
6121	Benz	29122	25176
6131	Benz	29135	23995
2219	Benz	29161	54825
3138	Benz	29163	43040
2261	Benz	29075	70217
6327	Benz	29137	87158
6126	Benz	29140	19648
6130	Benz	29138	37320
6124	Benz	29124	38247
2217	Benz	29139	117979
2264	Benz	29074	46454
6122	Benz	29113	48762
7517	Benz	29207	104196
7516	Benz	29224	76543
6145	Benz	29206	20652
6149	Benz	29170	81761
6140	Benz	29167	82685
6142	Benz	29162	45489
7502	Benz	29084	33112
7715	Benz	29240	43762
6147	Benz	29173	39097
7511	Benz	29214	39264
6135	Benz	29168	37190

Roland D.VI 6142/18

Roland DVI 7517/18 awaiting disposal

Albatros D.V at Coblenz

<u>Fifth Shipment listed in the order they arrived</u>

Alb. DV	6914/17	Mercedes 31336	118219 Essen
Fok. DVII	2178/18	Mercedes 12067	38022 Essen
Fok. DVII	5051/18	BMW 1519	38022 Essen
Alb. DV	5766/17	Mercedes 34888	118219 Essen
Fok. DVI	1655/18	Rotary 3186	37879 Essen
Alb. DII	1777/16	Mercedes 31821	37879 Essen
Pfalz DIIIa	5996/17	Mercedes 35852	37596 Essen
Alb. DIII	5138/17	Mercedes 34078	37596 Essen

Railroad car 18219 from Essen came with wings only.

Fok DVI	1639/18	Rotary 5955	44156 Berlin
Fok DVII	4350/18	Mercedes 42225	44156 Berlin
Rol DVIa	3620/18	Mercedes 24604	42779 Halle
Rol DVIa	3615/18	Mercedes 32022	42779 Halle
Alb DV	4698/17	Mercedes 35252	43503 Halle
Alb DVa	6530/	Mercedes 36150	43503 Halle
Alb DVa	5687/17	Mercedes 33149	43639 Berlin
Alb DV	7402/17	Mercedes 35181	119251 Essen

Railroad car 119251 from Essen also contained wings.

Alb DV	4656/17	Mercedes 34486	24587 Bromberg
Alb DIII	5070/17	Mercedes 33178	24587 Bromberg
Alb DV	7182/17	Mercedes 35376	39579 Hanover
Pfalz DXII	3470/17	Mercedes 41663	39579 Hanover
Alb DV	2360/17	Mercedes 35215	104042 Essen
Pfalz DIII	5906/17	Mercedes 34617	104042 Essen
Pfalz DIIIa	8054/17	Mercedes 36859	20756 Halle
Pfalz DIIIa	8190/17	Mercedes 37127	20756 Halle

Railroad car 45654 from Halle also contained wings.

Pfalz DIII	5862/17	Mercedes 35739	102771 Els-Loth
Alb DIII	2118/16	Mercedes 31110	102771 Els-Loth
Alb DVa	6802	Mercedes 27232	83363 Magdeburg
Alb DIII	5084/17	Mercedes 35991	83363 Magdeburg
Pfalz DIII	8293/17	Mercedes 32737	76087 Munchen
Alb DV	5808	Mercedes 36087	76087 Munchen
Alb DVa	7095/17	Mercedes 36793	70884 Breslau
Alb. DVa	5902	Mercedes 36109	70884 Breslau

Railroad car 30092 from Coln also contained wings

Halb DIII	138/16	(No Name) 502	56213 K Sach
(Used for flight test)			
Pfalz DVIII	159/18	Rotary 3626	23549 Bromberg
(4 blade propeller)			
Pfalz DXII	2485/18	Mercedes 41985	23549 Bromberg
Alb DIII	5055/17	Mercedes 34619	30338 Coln
Alb DV	3862	Mercedes 34113	30338 Coln
Railroad car 45950 from Wurtemberg also contained wings			
Pfalz DIII	8176/17	Mercedes 35917	42575 Berlin
Pfalz DIIIa	8181/17	Mercedes 36158	42575 Berlin
Railroad car 118706 from Essen also contained wings			
Pfalz DIIIa	5871/17	Mercedes 35709	37827 Essen
Pfalz DIIIa	8254	Mercedes 4887	37827 Essen
Railroad car 24010 from Konigsberg also had wings			
Fokker DR1	1877/17	Rotary 3549	41441 Berlin
To be used for flight testing			
Fokker DR1	1778/17	Rotary 25410	41441 Berlin
Alb DVa	6857/17	Mercedes 37410	28903 Coln
Alb DVa	2064/17	Mercedes 31860	28903 Coln
Alb DIII	5051/17	Mercedes 33883	36494 Essen
Fokker DR1	141/17	Rotary 3579	36494 Essen
Alb DIII	5051/17	Mercedes 34346	28300 Saarbrucken
(To be used for flight testing.)			
Alb DVIa	1233/18	Mercedes 29153	28300 Saarbrucken
Alb. DV	4561/17	Mercedes 33085	15448 Lothringian
Alb DV	5690/17	Mercedes 33016	15448 Lothringian
Pfalz DIII	8315/17	Mercedes 40799	28219 Saarbrucken
Alb DVa	5715/17	Mercedes 35511	28219 Saarbrucken
Fok DVII	587/18	Mercedes 42478	28411 Saarbrucken
Fok DVI	1676/18	Rotary 51551	28411 Saarbrucken
Alb DV	5399/17	Mercedes 37138	35549 Essen
Alb DVa	5287/17	Mercedes 33879	35549 Essen
Pfalz DIII	8021/17	Mercedes 35876	82494 Magdeburg
Alb DVa	5311/17	Mercedes 36045	

NOTE: Fokker D.VII (ex-German D7795/18) collided with a Martin NBS-1 over Langley Field, VA 6 Dec 1922, six killed. 8323 became 94040.

Albatros D.V at Coblenz awaiting transfer to the United States

Crashed Roland at Coblenz

Halberstadt C.V at Coblenz

Junkers J.I 586/18

Skull and Cross Bones Albatros

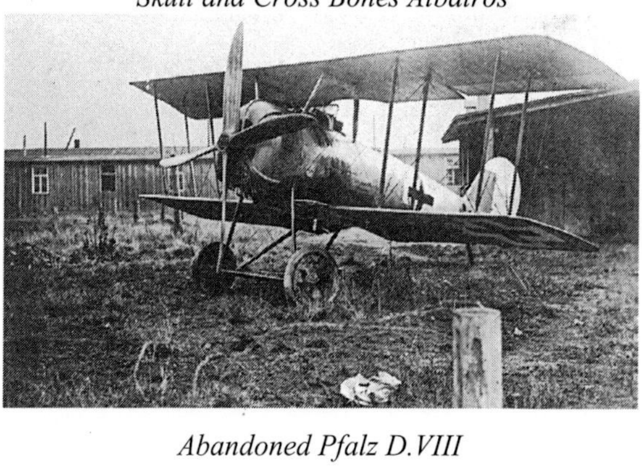

Abandoned Pfalz D.VIII

Fokker D.VII tested at McCook Field under a Project number

Project Number	German Serial	USAAS Serial	Disposition
P-108	7776/18		Shipped to Washington, D.C.,
			October 3, 1920
P-127	-	94040	Salvaged
P-138	-	94039	Surveyed September 25, 1922
P-143	-	94104	Transferred to Wright Field, Ohio,
P-144	-	94102	27, February 1922
P-195	-	64346	Surveyed September 2, 1922
P-210	5382/18	-	Salvaged November 5, 1923
P-212	2558/18	-	Surveyed November 5, 1924
P-213	6684/18	-	Transferred to Indianapolis,
P-228	-	68543	Indiana, April 29,1922
P-290	-	94034	Surveyed December 4, 1923
P-291	-	94104	Shipped to Fairfield, Ohio, January
			5, 1923
			Surveyed October 27, 1923
			Surveyed July 10, 1925

United States Army Air Service Fokker D.VII

ARMISTICE

11 November 1918

In addition to the difficulty arising out of the question of the presidency of the Commission, there had also been some uncertainty as to the military member, General Winterfeldt. President Wilson in his final note had stated that the Allied and Associated Powers would not treat with a representative of the Supreme Command but only with a delegate appointed by the German Government. Winterfeldt therefore was not a representative of the German Army but only a liaison between the Supreme Command and the Government: He had been chosen and appointed by Prince Max of Baden and not by Hindenburg. This circumstance was later seized on by the leaders of the Old Army as conclusive evidence that the Government and not the Army had sued for peace and that the Supreme Command was not therefore responsible for the severity of the Armistice terms!

Field Marshal Foch's train and carriage heading for the Armistice

The Commission arrived at Rethondes, near Compiegne, at 7 o'clock on the morning of 8 November and found awaiting them was Marshal Foch, General Weygand, Admiral Sir Rosslyn Weymss, and Admiral Hope. The negotiations were conducted in the Marshal's special train, where 22 years later the same scene was to be re-enacted but with the roles reversed.

Matthias Erzberger, Secretary of State, German delegate

Count von Obendorff second civilian delegate

General von Winterfield

General von Gundall

Staff car bearing a white flag leaves General Headquarters Spa 29 November 1918

Foch and the Entente delegation at the Armistice surrender carriage. To his right Admiral of the Fleet Sir Rosslyn Wemys

The German delegates were shown into the Marshal's work compartment shortly after 9 o'clock. They were received, "stiffly but courteously," by Weygand and Hope. A few minutes later Foch entered with Weymss and the Germans were presented. After the examination of the Germans' credentials, the delegates were seated; Foch between Weymss and Weygand, Erzberger opposite him with Oberndorff and Winterfeldt to his right and left.

"What is the purpose of your visit?" asked the Marshal, "What do you want of me?"

"We have come to receive the proposal of the Allied Powers toward the conclusion of an Armistice," Erzberger replied.

"I have no such proposals to make," said Foch coldly. Bewildered and disconcerted, the Germans sat speechless. Finally Count Obendorff broke the silence:

"M. le Marechal, how do you wish us to express ourselves? We are not fencing in words. We are ready to say that we desire the conditions of an Armistice."

"I have no conditions to give you," Foch repeated.

Erzberger began agitatedly to read the text of Wilson's final note, but the Marshal cut him short.

"If you want an Armistice, ask for it-formally."

"Yes, that is what we are asking for."

"Very well, we will read you the terms on which it can be granted."

Weygand then read the principal clauses of the agreement. Winterfeldt, during the reading, grew more and more disconsolate. Erzberger and Oberndorff maintained complete composure. Erzberger at once requested that military operations should be suspended immediately and the blockade raised. Revolution, he said, had broken out in Germany and he feared a spread of Bolshevism to Western Europe. The German Government needed freedom from Allied military pressure to restore discipline in the army and order at home.

Foch rejected the plea. "You are suffering from a loser's malady," he told the Germans. "I am not afraid of it. Western Europe will find the means to defend itself against Bolshevism."

Tableau représentant la signature de l'armistice de 1918 dans le wagon-salon du Maréchal Foch. Derrière la table, de droite à gauche, le général Weygand, le maréchal Foch (debout) et les amiraux britanniques Wemyss, G.Hope et J.Marriott. Devant, le ministre d'État allemand Matthias Erzberger, le général major Detlof von Winterfeldt (avec le casque) de l'armée impériale, le comte Alfred von Oberndorff des Affaires étrangères et le capitaine de vaisseau Ernst Vanselow de la Marine impériale. (Maurice Pillard Verneuil 1869–1942)

Adapted photograph, which depicts from left to right: German Admiral Ernst Vanselow, German Count Alfred von Oberndorff (1870 - 1963) of the Foreign Ministry, German army general Detlof von Winterfeldt, British Royal Navy Captain Jack Marriott (Naval Assistant to the First Sea Lord), Matthias Erzberger, head of the German delegation Center party member of the Reichstag (1875 - 1921), who was later murdered by Freikorps rightists for his role in the Armistice, British Rear-Admiral George Hope (Deputy First Sea Lord), British Admiral of the Fleet Sir Rosslyn Erskine Wester Wemyss (First Sea Lord), Marshal of France Ferdinand Foch (1851 - 1929), and French general Maxime Weygand (1867 - 1965). (B&W by GM A. MacKay)

Winterfeldt asked for time for a careful examination of the terms, and repeated the request for a suspension of hostilities, pointing out that should the struggle continue there would be many "...among the troops and the people, who will have fallen needlessly at the last moment and who might be preserved for their families."

The Marshal was adamant on this point: "Hostilities cannot cease before the signing of the Armistice." But he granted facilities of communication with the High Command at Spa, and von Helldorf was accordingly despatched with the terms of the Armistice. He was warned however that the original time limit of 72 hours set for consideration would not be extended. It would expire at 11 o'clock on the morning of 11 November 1918.

The observations of the German delegates were presented to Foch on the 9th. They contested none of the principal military and naval clauses but asked an extension of time in certain conditions connected with the withdrawal of troops and also for a decrease in the number of machine guns to be surrendered, on the grounds that the German Government would not have sufficient lcft to maintain order. They protested, however, that the maintenance of the blockade and the surrender of railway material were inhuman, as they would paralyze the means of feeding the population.

Foch granted few concessions. If the Germans had not sufficient machine guns they could use their rifles. As to the surrender of rolling stock, the Allies were demanding only such locomotives as the Germans themselves had taken from the French and Belgian people. In no case could the blockade be lifted, but the Germans were informed that they would be allowed to obtain supplies for their civil population. Erzberger regarded this as a major gain.

Finally, Foch granted 15 instead of 14 days for the evacuation of invaded territory, 31 days instead of 25 to complete the withdrawal and a reduction in the number of machine guns to be surrendered from 30,000 to 25,000.

10 November passed in anxiety and confusion. News arrived of the abdication of the Kaiser and of the establishment of a revolutionary government in Berlin. The German delegates were uncertain as to the validity of their credentials and Foch officially warned them at

6:30p.m. that they must sign on the morrow or not at all. At 8 p.m. came a radio-telegram in cypher from Hindenburg urging that if possible a modification on certain points should be obtained but adding that in any case the armistice convention must be signed. At 10:30 p.m. a further telegram arrived, in clear, from Berlin. The German Government accepted the conditions of the Armistice communicated to it on November 8.
THE IMPERIAL CHANCELLOR-3084. Erzberger explained that the number was a code figure to establish its authenticity. The Germans passed the first part of the night in discussion and at 2 o'clock intimated their readiness to sign. Yet a further 3 hours passed in a last vain effort to extract additional concessions and the convention was not signed until ten minutes past five on the morning of 11 November 1918.

(The Defeat of the German Army 1918, Special Service Division, Army Service Forces. 1947)

The Kaiser

Wilhelm II (Friedrich Wilhelm Viktor Albert; 27 January 1859 – 4 June 1941) was the last German Emperor (The Kaiser) and King of Prussia, reigning from 15 June 1888 until his abdication on 9 November 1918. Born during the reign of his great-uncle Frederick William IV of Prussia, Wilhelm was the son of Prince Frederick William and Victoria, Princess Royal. Through his mother, he was the eldest grandchild of Queen Victoria of the United Kingdom. In March 1888, Wilhelm's father ascended the German and Prussian thrones as Frederick III. Frederick died just 99 days later and his son succeeded him as Wilhelm II. Wilhelm's birth was very difficult and resulted in a damaged left arm. His mother insisted n the use of an English doctor. Due to the heavy use of anaesthetics during birth it was also felt that he suffered some minor brain damage. Moreover, at first the damaged arm appeared to be more than a local disability: the left leg reacted but slightly and the child suffered pain in the left ear and corresponding side of the head.

He was named Friedrich Wilhelm Victor Albrecht and called “Fritz” until he was six years old having been born in the Palace of Potsdam. Wilhelm's upbringing was strict and authoritarian. His

The Kaiser hunting in Great Britain

The Kaiser and Kaiserin

The Kaiser in uniform

The Kaiser in Turkey, second from the left, at the Dardanelles.

mother seemed to resent him, probably due to the circumstances of his birth. He was educated first at the Kassel Gymnasium and then at the University of Bonn. On attaining his majority, he was admitted into the Most Noble Company of the Black Eagle and at the same time he entered as a first lieutenant the First Regiment of Guards, in which at the age of ten he had begun his military career. He was a militarist and keen to expand the German Navy making it equal to the Royal Navy. Wilhelm II spent his early years at a school in Cassel on the River Main and showed the depth of his character frequently. There the senior instructor was an old sergeant of the Hessians and as part of the training he insisted on all boys having a swim in the River Main on regular days of the week. On one occasion Wilhelm refused point blank to enter the water and the sergeant instructor picked him up by his shirt collar and trousers and threw him in. Wilhelm, who was an honorary captain in a Berlin regiment, reported the matter to the Head of the School and also to his father and his grandfather, complaining that that the sergeant had assaulted a superior officer and demanded a suitable punishment. After some days the sergeant received a commission as a major, dated six months previously and was instructed to sentence the disobedient Captain Wilhelm to fourteen days C.B. (confined to barracks).

As a young man, Wilhelm fell in love with one of his maternal first cousins, Princess Elisabeth of Hesse-Darmstadt. She rejected his advances and married into the Russian imperial family. In 1880 Wilhelm became engaged to Augusta Victoria of Schleswig-Holstein, known as "Dona". They met when Wilhelm first saw her in the kitchen baking bread. The couple married on 27 February 1881 and they remained married for 40 years, until her death in 1921. In a period of 10 years, between 1882 and 1892, Augusta Victoria bore Wilhelm seven children, six sons and a daughter, Wilhelm, Eitel, Friedrich, Adalbert, August, Wilhelm, Oscar and Joachim and their one daughter Victoria Louisa. Strangely the children were not permitted to see the Emperor personally only through an intermediary and this was usually “Daddy Schulz” [his Chamberlain].

Wilhelm became emperor of Germany in 1888 following the death of his father Frederick II. At the time of his accession Otto von

With his daughter Princess Louise

Leaving General Headquarters

Kaiser Wilhelm II on parade with his sons, Wilhelm, German Crown Prince; Prince Eitel Friedrich, Prince Adalbert, Prince August Wilhelm, Prince Oskar, and Prince Joachim.(Joachim learned to fly at Johannisthal in 1915)

Bismarck was still German Chancellor; however he was effectively dismissed from office by Wilhelm II, two years later. The elderly Bismarck proved unable - or unwilling - to work with the new Kaiser. Wilhelm's foreign policy towards Britain and her Empire was by turns contradictory. In 1898 he travelled to the Holy Land in his yacht and visited Jerusalem and later, even visited the monastery at Monte Casino in Italy. The Kaiser was very comfortable with peoples of all faiths. In 1898 the Kaiser presented to the German Association of the Holy Land the plot of ground known as the "Dormition," acquired by him from the Sultan as a result of his pilgrimage to Jerusalem. It was his decision in 1906, that the Dormition should be administered by the Benedictine monks of Beuron Abbey.

He supported South Africa during the Second Boer War of 1899-1902 but he attempted a reconciliation shortly afterwards. He held a senior position within the British armed forces, he was in fact sixth inline to the British throne and he confessed that he could not envisage a war with Britain. Yet he publicly criticised King Edward VII after war was declared in August 1914, he wrote that war would never have occurred had Queen Victoria, who died in 1901, still held the British throne.

He completely misjudged the Austro-Hungarian attack on Serbia, in June 1914 which brought in France, Russia and Great Britain. The Emperor was Commander in Chief of the German military forces but as the war progressed he lost control to the German military warlords. The German military took control of all events resulting in the disastrous spring campaign of 1918 on the Western Front. Kaiser Wilhelm paid the price and abdicated fleeing to Doorn in the Netherlands with his family in the autumn of 1918…..

"The frontier was not far away. The cars drew up. The frontier-guard in his Dutch uniform refused to let German officers pass. His officer was sent for. For a moment he thought he must be dreaming; then he knew what to do: Telephone to The Hague. For the present he conducted the gentlemen to a little iron waiting-room. But before those at The Hague-the Ministers and the Queen-could make up their minds, six hours went by………

The Emperor with von Below

von Richthofen meets his Emperor

January 1919 ex-Kaiser at Doorn

The Kaiserin

Ex Kaiser in the grounds at Doorn 1921

At Doorn the ex-Kaiser and his family.

Wilhelm II with Princess Hermine Reuss of Greiz, 9 Novembe1922

...At last! The officer, saluting, comes into the waiting room. 'The gentlemen may pass.' With leaden heart the Emperor goes to his car; he even forgets, to-day, to hide his withered arm under his cape. A soldier sits in front, escorting the distinguished prisoners. The engine throbs-the car drives on into the alien land from which there will be no home-coming. Fainter, ever fainter. Soon the Emperor can scarcely hear the groaning of his land."

(KAISER WILHELM II by EMIL LUDWIG, G. P. PUTNAM'S SONS LTD. London, New York 1928)

At Doorn, in their new home, on 11 April 1921, the Kaiserin, Augusta Victoria passed away after a long and painful illness. Then Wilhelm received a birthday greeting from a son of the late Prince Johann George Ludwig Ferdinand August Wilhelm of Schönaich-Carolath. The 63-year-old Wilhelm invited the boy and his mother, Princess Hermine Reuss of Greiz, to Doorn where the Emperor found the 35-year-old Hermine a good companion and greatly enjoyed her friendship. The couple were married at Doorn on 5 November 1922 despite the objections of his supporters and his children. The Emperor said of her, *"Her approval is my pride, and sustains me; it allows me to laugh at hostile criticism. I write no sentence on religion or politics or science; I decide no personal problem without her advice. Her judgement is phenomenal. She manages her estates in Germany with the skill of a man. Her knowledge of practical affairs is infinitely greater than mine. Above all, she understands people. She has X-ray eyes. She can see through a man or a woman in a few minutes. The readiness with which she reads people's thoughts is positively uncanny."* Hermine's daughter, Princess Henriette, married the late Prince Joachim's son, Karl Franz Josef, in 1940, but divorced in 1946. Hermine remained a constant companion to the aging emperor until his death.

In great secrecy, his private art collection was sold off in the spring of 1929. Sir Joseph Duveen paid almost half a million pounds for six of the pieces. One of the most notable of his acquisitions was the famous Watteau, "*L'Embarquement pour Cythere,*" which depicts the French Court, attired as shepherds and shepherdesses, setting out to the island of Venus to follow their amorous pursuits. The figure mentioned as the purchase price was about £50000. The German people expressed the opinion that the paintings were not his but belonged to the people of Germany. After this he promised that if he was to sell the balance of his collection he would allow German museums or individuals to assess them before the sale.

Kaiser Wilhelm II of Germany died 4 June 1941 at Doorn at 1130 a.m. aged 82. In accordance with his wishes, the ceremony was private and only for members of his family; a delegation from the German Reich was expected to attend. Princess Hermine, his second wife and the Duchess of Brunswick, his only daughter, were among those at the death-bed. He was to be buried in the Cardinal Chapel at Doorn. He refused to be buried in Germany until the monarchy was restored.

The Crown Prince

Wilhelm, German Crown Prince, Crown Prince of Prussia (Friedrich Wilhelm Victor August Ernst; 6 May 1882 – 20 July 1951) was the eldest child of the last Kaiser, the German Emperor, Wilhelm II and his consort Augusta Victoria of Schleswig-Holstein. As Emperor Wilhelm's heir, he was the last Crown Prince of the German Empire and the Kingdom of Prussia. He became crown prince at the age of six in 1888, when his grandfather Frederick III died and his father became emperor. He was crown prince for 30 years until the collapse of the German Empire on 9 November 1918.

A great traveller in 1909 he visited England, Italy Egypt, Greece and Asia Minor. Later that year he travelled with his wife to Ceylon by way of Egypt to India where he was well received. There he enjoyed his love of hunting and sport. He was impressed by the decentralisation of government and how the officials were very young. At Peshawar he read in an English newspaper that His Majesty the Kaiser had appointed him to the command of his First Life Hussars at Langfuhr by Danzig. After his return to Germany he visited the courts of Rome, St Petersburg, Vienna and lastly attended the Coronation of George V at the Court of St James.

Crown Prince, centre July 1914

With William eldest son

April 1914

With the Emperor possibly Verdun

With General von Croda April 1918

Reviewing the troops

During the winter 1913-14 the Crown Prince was ordered to the Great General Staff for purposes of initiation and research. His instructor was Lieutenant-General Schmidt von Knobelsdorf, who later became his Chief of General Staff in the Upper Command of the Fifth Army. von Knobelsdorf was a brilliant teacher in tactics and strategy, his lectures and the themes he set for the prince were precise. von Knobelsdorf's chief maxim was: clearness of decision on the part of the leader ; translation of the decision into commands; leave your subordinates the widest scope of personal responsibility.

During the Great War, the prince commanded the 5th Army on the Western Front from 1914 to 1916 and was commander of the Army Group German Crown Prince for the remainder of the war. The Crown Prince's main explanation for the failure of the Battle of Verdun (February to December 1916) was that he had not enough men for his Fifth Army and they possessed little in the way of reserves. Schlieffen, in 1904 had laid the plan of attack and later it was Moltke's plan to attack France through Belgium. It was not the plan of Falkenhayn, then Minister of War. In fact Falkenhayn opposed it, suggesting a shorter front and a terrific drive through Verdun. The Kaiser made the decision to go ahead with the attack.

The Crown Prince was persuaded that Verdun would have fallen in 1914 and again at the beginning of 1916. But Falklanhayn's idea in 1915, which had been to attack Verdun as a diversion, without any definite intention of capturing it, was severely criticised by the Crown Prince and he objected to the casualties at Verdun. Probably this was why he was liked by his soldiers, he stood up for them and additionally he was an excellent man manager. But it was in 1915 that the Crown Prince concluded that Germany could never win the war time was in the hands of the Entente. He wanted peace through compromise

On 1 January 1915, a German officer advanced under a flag of truce to the French lines and handed over a packet to be given to the French Commander, General Sarrail who had pinned down the Crown Prince's Fifth Army in the vicinity of Verdun. The packet contained a photograph of the Crown Prince, with the words pencilled in German

The Prince and his staff car

At Verdun with General von Gallwitz

Army Group Headquarters June 1918

Sedan May 1917

In Exile Holland 26 December 1918

In Exile in Holland January 1919

Holland March 1919

The ex-Crown Prince and his wife

Post war the ex-Kaiser's family with the ex –Crown Prince centre

on the back-"General, - I wish my chivalrous enemy a happy New Year.-Wilhelm Crown Prince."

After events from August 1918 it was obvious the war was lost. On 8 November 1918 he was ordered to Spa to meet his father the Kaiser who was lodged in Villa Franeuse, just outside the town. After a deep discussion about the collapse of the front the Kaiser decided to go. Afterwards there was communicated to the various troops by wireless telegrams this declaration stating: *"The Kaiser and King has resolved to abdicate the throne. The Imperial Chancellor remains in office till the questions connected with the abdication of the Kaiser, the renunciation of the throne by the Crown Prince of the German Empire and of Prussia, and the appointment to the regency are settled. ..."* The army could not guarantee the Emperor's safety and the decision was taken to flee to Holland. On the evening of the eleventh November the Crown Prince laid down his command and proceeded to Holland following his father. The departure took place on the forenoon of the twelfth. On arrival at Holland the Dutch Government appointed the Isle of Wieringen as the Crown Prince's residence.

The Prince was an accomplished artist in charcoal and crayon, his drawings being used in the German First Army newspaper; sadly the newspaper plates were destroyed after the war. After his return to Germany in 1923, he fought against the Weimar Republic and campaigned for the reintroduction of the monarchy in Germany. His plan to become president of the German Republic was blocked by his father. When the National Socialists came to power, Wilhelm realised that Hitler had no intention of restoring the monarchy and their relationship became distant and cooled. Wilhelm became head of the House of Hohenzollern on 4 June 1941 following the death of his father Kaiser Wilhelm II and he held that position until his own death on 20 July 1951.

Prince William on his Indian Motor Cycle which he used to travel to Germany-at one point he crashed breaking a wrist and injuring himself

Friedrich Wilhelm Victor August Ernst;
German Crown Prince, Crown Prince of Prussia
6 May 1882 – 20 July 1951
(Image taken 1933)

Printed by Merchant City \Print
A Big City
North Britain